THE
WORKING
POOR

Kennikat Press
National University Publications
Interdisciplinary Urban Studies

General Editor

Raymond A. Mohl
Florida Atlantic University

DENNIS P. SOBIN

THE
WORKING
POOR

MINORITY WORKERS IN
LOW-WAGE, LOW-SKILL JOBS

NATIONAL UNIVERSITY PUBLICATIONS

KENNIKAT PRESS ● 1973

Port Washington, N.Y. ● London

Library of Congress Catalog Card No.: 73-83269
ISBN: 0-8046-9050-2

Manufactured in the United States of America

Published by
Kennikat Press, Inc.
Port Washington, N.Y./London

TO MY PARENTS,
FOR THEIR HELP AND FRIENDSHIP

CONTENTS

TABLES

THE
WORKING
POOR

1

INTRODUCTION: ISSUES AND ANSWERS

"I'm a shit." Thus did the black hospital orderly being interviewed by the author summarize the feelings he had about himself when he thought about his low–wage, low–skill job. The statement followed a half–hour conversation on the subject. He told all about it—what he did, how long he was doing it, how his supervisor treated him, and what his friends and family thought about his job.

Not long ago an unskilled worker with similar feelings wrote a book about his work and the way he felt about it. He painted pictures of the several menial jobs he had held. The pictures were not very pretty. They revealed the bitterness, hopelessness, and despair that such jobs can impart to those who perform them.

In one chapter entitled "The Mutilation of Man," the laborer–turned–author argued that much menial work can be done better by animals than by men. The argument was convincing. He made his point by showing the superiority of the watchdog over the watchman and the four–legged horse over the human work–horse.[1] The book's title was *The Making of a Moron*.

But the black hospital orderly interviewed did not think of himself as a moron, though he said that everybody was

3

treating him like one and that, indeed, the ingredients were there in his job to make him one someday. Coming to the end of our talk the worker continued to voice his criticisms. Although negative throughout, the conversation managed to end on a positive note. For we had finally touched upon a topic that the worker felt positive about. The topic was rioting.

This first came as a surprise. Here was a riot–prone ghetto inhabitant who was not unemployed. Quite the contrary. The man was working steadily in a secure civil service job. Yet the report of the National Advisory Commission on Civil Disorders (the Riot Commission) issued after the major urban riots of the late 1960's made clear that this seeming contradiction is common, and indeed understandable. The report pointed to the Commission's finding that "there are no substantial differences in unemployment between the rioters and the non-involved."[2]

But the Commission discovered some differences between rioters and nonrioters in employment—not in the rate of unemployment but in the types of jobs held. Rioters, the data showed, had jobs that gave least personal satisfaction, and the rioters that the Commission interviewed claimed that their dissatisfaction with their work was more than a matter of the small wages they received. They complained about such things as the small degree of responsibility involved in their work, the "dead–end" nature of their jobs, and their strong suspicion that racial discrimination rather than limited ability blocked the path to promotion.

The Commission concluded that the real employment problem in the ghetto is not so much the lack of work but the scarcity of economically and psychologically rewarding jobs. Thus the report stated: "Underemployment is an even more serious problem for ghetto residents than unemployment."[3] The implication was that a community is less prone to violent protest if its residents are without jobs rather than if the jobs held are menial, unrewarding, and dead–end.

When the Riot Commission's report was published it was said that few of its findings were truly original. For example, previous researchers and writers have found that a person's job can have an influence on his life after working hours. Harold Wilensky, for example, formulated a "compensatory leisure hypothesis." His hypothesis is that violence and aggression is often a form of compensation for repetitive and unrewarding work. He gives the following example:

> An assembly-line worker, for eight hours gripped bodily to the main line, doing repetitive, low-skilled, machine-paced work which is wholly ungratifying, comes rushing out of the plant gate, helling down the superhighway at 80 miles-an-hour in a second-hand Cadillac Eldorado, stops off for a beer and starts a bar-room brawl, goes home and beats his wife, and in his spare time throws a rock at a Negro moving into the neighborhood.[4]

Others have also noted the possibility of the far–reaching importance of work on a person's life. Recently, as social commentators and behavioral scientists have become concerned with the plight of impoverished minorities and the rising tide of social problems in their communities, the subject of work has received much attention. In search of solutions for these social ills, it is often pointed out that a primary need is to increase both the number and quality of jobs. The aggregate number of jobs is important to help break the "cycle of poverty"—the perpetuation of impoverishment from generation to generation. The quality of jobs is important because most jobs that are now available to the poor are of such a lowly and unrewarding nature that they often contribute to the "culture of poverty"—a community climate of frustration, anxiety, and despair.

The low–wage, low–skill, dead–end jobs that are available to ghetto residents seem to contribute to a wide range of problems for them. Besides those of a social, psychological, and political nature, such work also contributes to economic problems, including poverty and even unemployment. These jobs represent a false hope for overcoming the problem of poverty. The 1972 *Manpower Report of the President* stated, "Included among the poor is a significant proportion of families whose heads work full time throughout the year but who still do not earn enough to lift themselves and their dependents above the poverty level."[5] Three economic researchers reported recently that not only does a large proportion of available jobs have little effect on poverty but they often help to perpetuate it. They stated:

> When great numbers of young workers are unable to earn enough to support wives and children in basic decency, they become demoralized and families fall apart and the welfare rolls soar. Property is not kept up, because it cannot be. Neighborhoods deteriorate, the circle of poverty and despair closes on itself and it eventually creates an enormous drag on the entire economy.[6]

The problem of unemployment is also hardly on its way to being solved by unskilled, low–paying job opportunities. "The slackened growth in the Negro labor force in 1971," according to the *Manpower Report of the President* previously mentioned, "was the outcome largely of a decline in participation rates, particularly among teenagers." The report continued, "There are indications that some Negro youth were deterred from entering the job market because of discouragement over job prospects."[7]

The Issues

The author of this book undertook research in order to discover the extent and nature of the impact that menial, low–paying jobs have on the lives of people—socially, economically, psychologically, and politically. The main goal of the research was to determine whether the jobs held by unskilled ghetto residents are helping or hindering them to solve their problems.

The research was designed to determine whether there is a correlation between the behavior and attitudes of people in their work situation and their attitudes and behavior away from the job. Of particular interest was the question of whether attitudes and behavior that originate in the work setting show up in some way after work hours.

The research addressed itself to several specific questions.

One of these was the question of whether minority people in low–level jobs are content with what they are doing. Do they aspire to or expect better jobs in the future? How affected are the lives of those who are dissatisfied with their work and who see their chance of obtaining better work as remote?

A specific concern of the research was the after–work activities of ghetto residents and the degree to which these seem to be influenced by their nine–to–five routine. The after–work activities examined were in the area of family affairs, social relations, and participation in community organizations. The political attitudes and participation of ghetto residents employed in low–skill jobs were also examined.

Another concern of the research was the reactions of the working poor to the poverty conditions in which they live. Do their jobs help or hamper their adjustment to their impoverished problem–plagued community environment? Since some of the research for this book was done in the late 1960's shortly after the major urban riots of that decade occurred, the topic of urban protest and group violence was also considered. Because the focus of the research was on the employed ghetto resident, particular attention was given to the role individuals in this situation have played in such occurrences. Beyond looking at the actual participation of the working poor in riots, an examination was made of their proneness to engage in disorders as revealed by their attitudes toward riots and the treatment that they felt should be given to rioters.

The preceding section of this chapter discussed some of the issues to which this book addresses itself. In order to study these issues, various types of information had to be gathered. Different research methods and sources of information were used, as discussed in the following section.

The Answers

Many of the conclusions contained in this book are based on a questionnaire survey which the author conducted of 108 unskilled black workers in public and private employment in Newark, Baltimore, and Cleveland. A description of the workers, their employers, and the cities in which they lived appear in Chapter 2. The people interviewed were employed in seven organizations chosen for a series of Federally supported job training programs. The interviews were conducted as part of a larger study sponsored by the U.S. Department of Labor in which the author also participated.

A questionnaire containing 350 questions was used to interview the workers. Each interview took up to two hours to complete. The first 250 questions concerned items required by the Department of Labor study, while the last 100 questions were developed by the author in accordance with his own research interests. About 90 percent of the questions were structured, requiring the interviewees to select one of several choices provided. These questions and some of the open–ended questions requiring sentence responses were subsequently coded and subjected to electronic data processing.

The 100 questions developed by the author called for the subjects to provide information about their jobs and their attitudes and activities away from the job, ranging from family affairs to community participation.

Before analyzing the results of the interviews, a preliminary inspection of the data was made. It revealed that not all of the workers interviewed were truly representative of the working poor. In contrast to six of the seven organizations, in which the workers earned from $50.00 to $90.00 per week and had an average educational level of less than high school completion, the workers in the other organization were paraprofessionals who earned upwards of $100.00 per week and had at least completed high school. Rather than discard the 32 workers in the paraprofessional group, the author used them for purposes of comparison with the 76 low–skill workers. If indeed workers with low–skill, dead–end jobs show distinctive patterns in their lives away from the job, here was an opportunity to examine this comparatively. By comparing the answers given by these workers to the answers of the higher–

level workers, some conclusions might be made regarding characteristics particular to the lower–level group.

It was also found upon preliminarily examining the data that about half of the low–skill workers were employed in hospitals and half worked in private plants. To be exact, there were 44 hospital workers and 32 plant workers. It was decided that these two groups should be compared to each other since other studies suggest that there might be some differences in the adjustment of low–skill workers to their jobs depending on the type of employing organization. In one study, it was found that workers identify with the objective or end product of their work and that their awareness of what it is and their opinion of its value to society influences the satisfaction they find in their job.[8] In view of this finding, it was assumed that the hospital workers would be better adjusted to their work than the plant workers. By comparing the two groups of workers this assumption could be tested.

After conducting the interviews the resulting information was analyzed in the following manner. Statistical tables were developed to compare the 32 paraprofessionals to the 76 low–skill workers. Other tables were developed to compare the 44 low–skill hospital workers to the 32 low–skill plant workers. A final set of tables cross–tabulated the answers given by workers who said they were satisfied with their work and those by workers who said that they were not satisfied, to see whether the two groups differed. Also, the answers of union members and nonmembers were compared to see if union membership made a difference.

In addition to the data obtained from the interview survey, other sources of information were studied. These included previous statistical surveys (both published and unpublished), government reports on employment patterns and ghetto conditions, books, and articles (both in professional journals and popular magazines). The materials used as part of this study served to provide background discussion both to introduce and interpret the survey results.

A final research approach was used. This was a survey

of noted authorities and public officials. People interviewed included professionals involved in manpower research, job training programs, and black community affairs. Many useful insights were obtained and help in locating published material, particularly the more obscure sources which might have been otherwise overlooked.

2

THREE CITIES, SEVEN EMPLOYERS, 108 BLACK WORKERS

With the objectives and approach of the book presented in the preceding chapter, the present chapter will deal with the cities in which the interview survey of workers was conducted, the 108 workers who comprised the sample, and the places where they were employed.

Three Urban Settings

The interviews were conducted in three cities: Baltimore, Maryland; Cleveland, Ohio; and Newark, New Jersey. These cities were those chosen by the U.S. Department of Labor for a series of experimentation and demonstration job training programs conducted in conjunction with this study.

The Department of Labor made its selection after looking at many cities. Factors considered were population characteristics, industrial and labor composition, ongoing manpower programs, and sociopolitical conditions. It is significant that the three cities selected had recent histories of social and political unrest. Each had been the scene of riots that had made national headlines in the late 1960's.

Baltimore, the largest of the cities, had a 1970 population of 905,759; it is slightly larger than Cleveland (750,903) and more than twice the size of Newark (382,417).

TABLE 1
STATISTICAL FEATURES OF BALTIMORE, CLEVELAND, AND NEWARK, 1970

	Baltimore	Cleveland	Newark
Total Population	905,759	750,903	382,417
Black Population	420,210	287,841	207,458
Land Area (Sq. Miles)	78	76	24
Population Density (Per Sq. Mile)	11,568	9,893	16,273
Population Change (1960-70)	—3.6%	—14.3%	—5.6%
Median Age (Years)	28.7	28.7	25.9
Population over 65	10.6%	10.6%	8.0%

Newark, with a population density of 16,273 per square mile, is the most urban of the three cities; the other two have about one–third less density. Like urban areas elsewhere, all three cities have been losing residents fleeing to relocate in outlying areas. This trend has been greatest in Cleveland, with a decline in population of 14.3 percent from 1960 to 1970, compared with the declines in Baltimore and Newark of 3.6 and 5.6 percent, respectively.

The most prosperous of the three cities is Baltimore, as evidenced by data on family income, employment rates, and housing conditions. Baltimore has the highest percentage of white collar employment. In addition, a higher percentage of its residents earned over $10,000 per year than in the other two cities.

The percentage of blacks in each of the three cities is high, and on the increase. Newark, with the highest, showed percentages of 17 in 1950, 34 in 1960, and 54 in 1970. The same trend, although less pronounced, has occurred in the other two cities.

TABLE 2
PERCENTAGE OF BLACKS IN BALTIMORE, CLEVELAND, AND NEWARK

	1950	1960	1970
BALTIMORE	24%	35%	46%
CLEVELAND	16%	29%	38%
NEWARK	17%	34%	54%

Source: U.S. Department of Commerce, Bureau of the Census

Many problems exist in these cities. One public official, Manuel Diaz of the U.S. Equal Employment Opportunity Commission, recently said: "Newark is the most dramatic situation —negatively—I've run into in terms of equal opportunity."[1] Nathan Wright, in a study of Newark, remarked that the city "in recent years is distinguished by an unexcelled list of firsts in urban pathology."[2] He cited Newark as leading the nation's cities in the following particulars: crime rate, tuberculosis rate, syphilis rate, gonorrhea rate, maternal mortality rate, proportionate urban tax rate, population density, proportion of land set aside for urban renewal clearance, and daytime population turnover.

Wright describes Newark's employment situation for blacks as very bad. He points out that although 80 percent of Newark's jobs are white collar, only 3.7 percent of them are held by blacks, who make up 54 percent of the population. Wright looked into the jobs held by Newark blacks in Federal government offices, an area of employment reputed to exemplify equal opportunity. He found that blacks fill only 14 percent of such Newark jobs. Wright also gathered data on workers employed by Newark's twenty–one largest companies. Their work force, his data showed, was only 10.5 percent black. More startling than this finding was that the proportion of blacks in these companies has remained about the same over the last several years. This indicates that relatively few blacks have been able to rise beyond entry–level positions.

Overall economic and employment trends in Newark have shown a steady decline. In 1909, for example, Newark's employment force was 20 percent of that of the state of New Jersey. By 1939 this proportion was down to 11 percent. In the war years, some major industries in Newark located elsewhere and the city lost many millions of dollars in assessed valuation along with several thousand jobs. Since the war a steady movement of factories to suburban areas has occurred.

The suburbs of Newark, which now offer many well paying jobs, are all but closed to blacks. Not being able to live in the suburbs because of their poverty and racial discrimination, Newark's blacks find it difficult to take advantage of the job opportunities there. During the war, when the munitions plants in suburban Morris County had to increase their production greatly, special buses were provided to carry black workers 40 to 50 miles from the Newark ghettos to the plants.

As white residents and industry fled to the suburbs, there was a steady flow of rural Southern blacks into the ghettos. This has resulted in even greater crowding into slum housing and increased competition for the low–paying, menial jobs available for the unskilled.

Cleveland became the oil center of the nation in the late 19th century after one of the Rockefellers established the Standard Oil Company there. A period of growth and prosperity ensued, making the city the fifth largest in the nation at the beginning of the 20th century.

In recent years, however, Cleveland has shared the problems of other major U.S. cities. Through in–migration of blacks and out–migration of whites and industry, its population has become increasingly black and progressively poorer. At the same time, problems of health, crime, and unemployment have been growing, reaching record proportions.

The 1970 census uncovered many alarming trends in the city. The percentage of black families below the poverty level had increased significantly in Hough and Kinsman, two of Cleveland's worst ghettos. At the same time that poverty had increased in black areas, a decrease had occurred in white areas. The separation between blacks and whites had widened.

In 1967 Carl B. Stokes, the first black to be chosen chief executive of a major U.S. city, was elected Cleveland's fiftieth mayor. The impact of his administration has still to be measured. But local government in Cleveland has regularly been ineffectual in dealing with the city's many problems. In some cases it has acted to worsen them. This seems to be true of the housing situation in Cleveland. Many critics claim that the failure of urban renewal there was due to the fact that the city–designed program was overly ambitious, inadequately planned, and poorly implemented. Some urban renewal sites after being cleared had not undergone rebuilding after ten years. The U.S. Department of Housing and Urban Development, which channels federal funds into urban renewal projects, was finally forced in 1967 to cut off support to Cleveland.

In Baltimore, one of the oldest cities between North and South, the mixed regional flavor is still apparent. Once an area relatively inactive and slow to change, it has been fairly progressive in recent years.

A substantial amount of physical redevelopment has taken place. A major rebuilding project completed a few years ago replaced twenty–two acres of deterioration in the city's downtown area with Charles Center, a complex consisting of nine office buildings and several hundred housing units in a few well–designed high–rise apartment structures. The project has become nationally recognized as a highly successful urban revitalization effort.

Yet this and other projects have barely begun to make an impact on the city's several problems. In 1970 approximately one out of five housing units was judged substandard by federal census officials. A major problem is the difficulty Baltimore has experienced in generating economic growth and maintaining population stability. The city sustained a population loss of 4 percent between 1960 and 1970.

One problem can be traced to the city's part–Southern heritage. Until recently, outright discrimination in restaurants and other public places was common. Today, racial imbalance exists largely in a *de facto* form. For example, 84 percent of all black elementary school children attend schools where less than 10 percent of the pupils are white.

The rate of unemployment in Baltimore in recent years has approached the national highs reached in Los Angeles and San Francisco. Estimates of unemployment in the city's ghettos indicate that the problem is concentrated there, with upwards of 15 percent of the labor force unemployed.

It can be seen that the three cities in which the present study was made are not untypical in terms of problems and

physical and social composition. Indeed they have many problems. And in each the problems appear to place the greatest
burden on black ghetto residents.

Seven Places of Employment

The 108 black workers who were interviewed as part of
this study were employed in seven organizations: two in Baltimore, two in Cleveland, and three in Newark. Three of the
employers were hospitals, three were manufacturing firms, and
one was a city agency. One hospital and one manufacturing
firm were located in each of the three cities, and the city
agency was in Newark.

The Newark agency had been a department of the city
government since 1938. Its primary responsibility was to provide "decent, safe, and sanitary" low–rent public housing. To
help stem the recent flight of middle–class residents to the
suburbs, this agency also became involved in developing
middle–income cooperatives and garden apartments. It has
also been a prime advocate of educational, cultural, entertain-
ment, and health centers to improve living in the city for low–
income residents. The agency is also the relocation and redevelopment arm of the city. The black workers interviewed
as part of this survey worked in the division (one of five) that
provided social services to residents in public housing projects.

In addition to providing such social services, the division
handled community relations for the agency. In this role it
was responsible for working with other community agencies
in developing special programs to meet the needs of housing
project residents. The division serviced about 40,000 people
living in 10,721 apartment units in 17 low–rent housing projects scattered throughout Newark. All the division's employees
were under the civil service system, with appointments to
permanent positions made from certification lists after exami-
nations.

The Newark hospital, with some 8,000 patients a month,
had the largest caseload of any general hospital in New Jersey.

The hospital was established in 1882 and became the first facility in Newark to provide health services to the indigent sick. The hospital's usual image had not been very good. It had at various times received nationwide attention for its problems of sanitation, accreditation, community criticism, and poor working conditions. It had even been labeled by Newark residents "the butcher shop on the hill."

But the hospital and its image recently underwent some change. One reason was a merger with a New Jersey medical school. At the time of this study, construction was underway for a major facility in Newark to serve as a new location for the hospital and a center for teaching and research facilities, clinical medicine, and administrative offices.

Employees working for the hospital totaled 1,674; approximately 70 percent women. Low–skilled workers were estimated at 200, most being in clerical and aide positions. Blacks comprised 44 percent of the hospital work force.

The private Newark firm in the study manufactured varied electronic products, including master and closed circuit T.V. equipment, community antenna systems, and electronic testing equipment. The company, a pioneer in the television industry, was established in 1949. It was considered at one time to be the biggest supplier of converters in the country. Company operations at the time of the study were carried out in four Newark plants within a two–mile radius. The main plant was a somewhat obsolete two–story building. It was old and overcrowded, and the noise level from heavy machinery was high. No cafeteria or eating room was provided. Most employees spent their lunch hour eating at their work station.

Approximately 500 workers were employed by this manufacturing concern. There was just one shift. Almost all of the workers performed unskilled or semi-skilled jobs. Although no figures were available from management, a high percentage of black and Spanish–speaking workers were observed in the production areas. The majority of low–skilled workers were women.

The Baltimore hospital where workers were interviewed was a private institution founded in 1854. It had been a segregated facility for most of its history. Only recently had it abolished discrimination against black patients. A wide range of services was offered by the hospital. An estimated 12,500 patients were admitted each year, while an additional 35,000 were treated in the emergency department.

The hospital was housed at the edge of a black ghetto in several old buildings, all somewhat obsolete and overcrowded. To alleviate overcrowding, the hospital had purchased and was using nearby row houses. An ambitious $18 million fund drive to build new facilities was nearing completion at the time of the study. Although the hospital originally intended to use this money to establish itself in a suburb, the Board of Directors approved plans to remain at its present location and to expand its medical services to better serve community needs. Approximately 1,200 full–time and part–time employees worked for the hospital, almost 500 of them low–skilled workers. Some 42 percent of the workers were black.

The private Baltimore establishment in the study was a meat processing plant that began operating in 1951. It had originally operated out of an empty branch building of a local dairy. The initial work force team of four doubled as production, sales, and clerical personnel. The company made steady progress and achieved an A–1 rating from Dun and Bradstreet. At the time of the study it was in a million dollar plant on a four–acre site in an industrial park. A wing completed in 1969 added to the production and office space.

The main plant building was completely modern and specifically designed for meat processing. The production area was maintained at 32° F., while one storage area for cooked meats was kept at the much lower temperature of –10° F. Because of such low temperatures, the plant was not a comfortable working environment. The plant was kept spotlessly clean. The company employed 150 workers; 95 worked in the main plant and the remainder were sales personnel who operated out of branch offices. Low–skilled workers represented about 56 percent of the labor force. Black workers comprised 85 percent of the employees.

The Cleveland hospital studied was a large, short–term general facility founded as a city institution in 1837. It contained more than 500 beds and a large out–patient clinic. Several years ago it affiliated with a major medical school in Ohio to become one of the largest teaching hospitals in the country, providing instruction in 26 medical specialties and subspecialties.

Hospital facilities consisted of 15 buildings on 25 acres. Housed were research laboratories, nursing and medical schools, an out–patient clinic, and one of the few remaining tuberculosis clinics in the city. Hospital employees numbered about 2,300, of whom almost 800 were low–skilled service workers. An additional 300 filled low–skilled clerical jobs. The racial composition of the work force was 75 percent black, 1 percent Puerto Rican, and 24 percent white. Approximately 75 percent of the workers were women.

The Cleveland manufacturing firm in the study produced lighting fixtures. It was established in 1923 and operated until recently as an independent firm. Prior to World War II, the principal products were chandelier–type lighting fixtures for private homes. During the war it manufactured lighting fixtures for the Army, Navy, and defense plants. Later it dropped out of the residential market and concentrated on the industrial trade, particularly schools, hospitals, and motels.

In 1961, the company merged with another. A few years later the merged company was purchased by a corporation employing 375,000, one of the largest in the nation, but the manufacturing operation in Cleveland was kept relatively intact. There were 200 workers employed in the plant, 85 percent low–skilled. The plant building was an old, multilevel structure. Many of the working conditions were found to be very poor. In the spray painting department, for example, despite a ventilation system, fumes were almost unbearable. The toilet rooms were so dirty that they clearly represented a health hazard.

108 Black Workers

The worker survey conducted as part of this study consisted of interviews with 108 black workers in the seven organizations described. Seventy–six were employed in unskilled jobs in the hospitals and plants. The remaining thirty–two workers held paraprofessional jobs in the city agency in Newark. The unskilled plant and hospital workers interviewed ranged from eight to fifteen for each organization.

The thirty–two paraprofessionals were community service aides, a civil service position that paid a starting salary of $110 per week. The job, a relatively new one in the agency, was created through the efforts of New Careers, an organization active throughout the country in attempting to establish public and private paraprofessional positions. The job of community service aide entailed some of the duties formerly performed by community service workers, the full professionals in the agency. One duty of the aide was to counsel ghetto residents on housing problems, particularly those brought about by the displacement and relocation resulting from urban renewal projects. The aide also was responsible for assisting residents of public housing projects in obtaining food, clothing, and medical assistance. Other duties involved designing and carrying out programs for children and teenagers in housing projects and planning special events such as trips to parks and museums. Finally, the aides served as liaison between the housing manager and the public housing occupants. They listened to the complaints of residents and sought to have their problems resolved by communicating them to the housing manager. These and other duties were clearly of a paraprofessional nature and might indeed have been considered fully professional if it were not for the fact that the community service workers closely supervised the community service aides.

These paraprofessionals were required to have a high school diploma, although no previous experience was necessary. They were also required to pass a civil service examination, although they could be appointed provisionally to their jobs and take the exam later. After passing the examination, they were certified as permanent civil service employees and given all the rights and privileges that this entailed.

The seventy–six unskilled workers in the study were employed in various menial jobs. Most of them were paid on an hourly basis. Their wages ranged from $1.25 to $2.40 per hour. The fringe benefits they were given were minimal. Most of them were not even covered by company health or pension plans.

The workers in the Newark hospital were largely unskilled clerical workers holding the positions of medical record clerk, clerk–typist, and file clerk. They worked in the medical records department in maintaining the files of patients.

In the Newark plant, the unskilled workers interviewed worked on an assembly line. Their jobs carried such titles as line operator, repair girl, line assembler, coil winder, relief girl, and utility operator. All were on a regular daytime shift.

The workers in the Baltimore hospital held jobs in the cafeteria. Their job titles were dishwasher, pantry aide, nourishment aide, and kitchen helper. Since these jobs required little skill and minimal training, the workers often performed them interchangeably.

In the Baltimore meat processing plant, the workers were in production. They worked on various meat processing machines or assisted in moving materials from one work station to another. Some worked on packing the final products for shipment. Their titles were machine operator, stuffer operator, smoker, floorman, and packer.

The workers employed by the Cleveland factory worked either on one of the assembly lines or in the stockroom. The assembly line positions were cleaner, assembler, punch press operator, spray painter, assistant metal cutter, and laborer. In the stockroom the workers held the jobs of shipping helper, order filler, and stock clerk.

The Cleveland hospital workers held basic maintenance positions. Their jobs carried the titles of porter and curtain hanger. Some of the porters were responsible for general floor and wall cleaning, while others were assigned to clean the equipment in the hospital.

Most of the 108 workers interviewed were female (61.1%), with a greater percentage of the paraprofessionals (81.2%) than of those in the unskilled group (52.6%). The largest number of workers were married and living with the spouse (42.6%); only about one out of four had never married (26.8%). The remaining 30.6 percent were either widowed, divorced, or separated. About 53 percent of the paraprofessionals and 38 percent of the unskilled workers were currently married and living with the spouse.

TABLE 3
MARITAL STATUS OF WORKERS INTERVIEWED

	Unskilled Workers		Para-professionals		Total	
Married and living with spouse	29	38.2%	17	53.1%	46	42.6%
Never Married	23	30.3%	6	18.7%	29	26.8%
Widow	3	4.0%	4	12.5%	7	6.5%
Divorced	8	10.5%	3	9.4%	11	10.2%
Separated	13	17.1%	2	6.3%	15	13.7%
Total	76	100%	32	100%	108	100%

Most of the workers in the survey (55.6%) reported that they were the main support of their family. This was about equal among the paraprofessionals and the unskilled workers. The next largest group of workers were those who worked along with their spouse to support the family.

TABLE 4
MAIN SUPPORT IN WORKER'S FAMILY

Main Support Of Family	Unskilled Workers		Para-professionals		Total	
Respondent	42	55.3%	18	56.3%	60	55.6%
Spouse	9	11.8%	12	37.5%	21	19.4%
Both Spouse and Respondent	5	6.6%	2	6.3%	7	6.5%
Parents	3	4.0%	0	0	3	2.8%
Brother or Sister	16	21.1%	0	0	16	14.8%
Other	1	1.3%	0	0	1	.9%
Total	76	100%	32	100%	108	100%

3

PEOPLE AND JOBS

Most behavioral scientists and social commentators agree that work occupies an important place in both the structure of society and in the lives of its individual members. Indeed, a substantial amount of time and effort is spent during a normal lifetime performing one's occupation. Depending on the type of occupation, years of preparation may also be involved.

Work is clearly a major human endeavor. As such, it has substantial and far-reaching implications.

The Human Meaning of Work

Different views have been expressed on the importance of work in society. Most of these views are based on factual evidence of one kind or another resulting from a multitude of studies. A common conclusion is that work is a key value in society.

The many studies of the psychological consequences of being out of work support this conclusion. Gainful employment is more than an individual goal; it is a mandate by society. As such, the pressures on people to pursue employment and, once obtained, remain employed, are enormous.

A study of automation and its impact on future employment disclosed that the degree of automation anticipated will permit most of the goods and services needed by society to be produced without human labor. The author recognized that this prospect of life without work could be a major social problem. He recommended that society anticipate this situation and seriously attempt to find "alternatives for work and production as basic goals."[1]

In a study of retirement interviews both with workers nearing retirement and with retirees were reported. Retirement, concluded the study, is an ordeal that most workers dread. And, indeed, when it does occur, major adjustment problems are often attendant. The average retiree in the study was not happy with his leisure life and was plagued with attitudes of helplessness and despair.[2]

A team of sociologists in the 1930's analyzed the attitudes and behavior of people living in a town hard hit by the depression and widespread unemployment. They noted:

> The crowd on the street moves with less firmness and purpose, cordiality goes out of many associations, people linger on corners, not relaxed as in leisure and not intent as in work. A community in the depths of unemployment lives in an atmosphere of lassitude and disinterest.[3]

In another study workers were asked whether they would continue to work if they had a source of income independent of their job. They said, by and large, that they would. Of particular interest is the fact that this answer was generally given regardless of the job held. The study concluded that for most people a job serves other functions than earning a living. Of greater importance is the feeling a job gives one of being a part of society, of having a purpose in life. Quoting from the study's conclusion, work "serves to anchor the individual into society."[4]

It is interesting to note that for most individuals, commitment to working is much deeper than commitment to their particular job. Clearly, work has a *social* importance—it is important to people because it is important to society. As with other forms of socially prescribed behavior, people feel compelled to work regardless of the personal satisfaction they derive from their particular job.

Two psychologists studying human adjustment found it impossible to separate occupational adjustment from general life adjustment. Thus they observed that job satisfaction seems to be a major component of overall contentment with life. Their data disclosed that the meaning a job has is influenced by whether the person is a man or a woman. They concluded that "work is a less important factor in the lives of women than it is for men."[5] The explanation offered is that greater family pressures and social expectations seem to be placed on males.

Tracing the meaning of work in history, it is clear that work has long been a central life interest for adults in most societies, and particularly in the Western world. It is also clear that since the beginning of civilization, people have been accorded stature largely on the basis of their work skills and the application of them to producing goods and services valued by society. Likewise, in most societies occupation has been a major determinant of social class position.

Questioning workers reveals than one's job is important because, among other things, it greatly determines the way others see him and, in turn, the way he sees himself. In other words, the work one does is often the most important source of self–identity. The question "Who is he?" most often means "What does he do—what is his job?" One's work therefore seems to identify a person in our culture more clearly than any other single characteristic.

In the light of what has been said, it is easy to jump to the conclusion that money is of secondary importance in encouraging people to work. Can this be true? What about the economic constraints that we often think bind people to their jobs? Is it not true that many workers, particularly those with unattractive jobs, work in order to support themselves and their families?

A survey of workers looked into these questions. It was

indeed found that most workers held their jobs as an economic necessity. There was little question that without their weekly check the workers could not support themselves and their families. Yet the researchers investigated further and found that marriage was considered important to the workers because, in the words of many of those questioned, "it provides a man with a family for whom he may work."[6] Even this study, therefore, presents a conclusion in line with the finding of others that the importance of a job goes well beyond the money derived from it.

Recalling that an enormous amount of time and energy is spent preparing for and then functioning in the world of work, the conclusion that work has far greater importance than is often realized should not be surprising. Not only is one's job taken seriously while it is being performed, but it is important away from the work place as well. Consider the fact that people often talk about their job when among family and friends. This is more common among white–collar workers than it is for manual workers. But although blue–collar workers normally talk little about their work in their nonwork time, it has been found that when forced by illness to be absent from work for a few days, their thoughts and conversation usually turn to the job.[7]

There is, therefore, overwhelming evidence that work is a central value in society and a key concern of its members. The implications of work and the reactions of people to their particular jobs are far–reaching.

The Effects of the Job on Nonwork Activities

The best way to appreciate the importance of work is to consider the pervasive influence it has on a person's total life. First, we must determine the impact of work on one's nonwork activities.

Among byproducts of a job that affect behavior after hours are friendships, techniques in interpersonal relations, prejudices, attitudes toward public issues, and even personality traits. Consider job–influenced personality characteristics and their effect on off–the–job behavior. Nervous habits or authoritarian tendencies can often be linked to the job situation. On a more general level the work experience often plays a major role in determining emotional well–being. Rather than economic security, psychological security seems to be a major work derivative. A feeling of security results from knowing that one's contribution is useful and that one is personally wanted and needed in his current job. In this way a job makes an important contribution to one's overall emotional stability.

Although the degree of emotional security derived from one's job varies with the adjustment and satisfaction experienced, the very fact that one has a steady job serves as a personal stabilizing force. A study covering five factories and numerous jobs showed that people who worked for a long period at a particular job felt very secure psychologically. So comfortable were they that regardless of whether the job, the work place, or the shift were desirable, they consistently stated their preference to have things as they were rather than make any changes. The reason given by the subjects was simply: "I am used to it."[8] In the same study the workers interviewed were asked their feelings about any changes they might desire in their lives outside of work. Workers long employed at the same job and reluctant to change their work situation expressed the same attachment to prevailing conditions away from the job. Few expressed a desire, for example, to move from their community, regardless of its quality or the number of shortcomings they felt it had.[9]

The several studies appear to agree that people's personalities and their psychological well–being are in part shaped by their work experience. A concluding comment is provided by one writer: "Industry feeds back into the community people whose personalities reflect their experience at work." He goes on to say: "Through its influence on the character of men and women, industry is fundamentally affecting the institutions, organizations, and groups in the community."[10]

Several of the many studies of the symptoms and causes of personal maladjustment have considered the possible effects of on–the–job experiences. Further evidence of the presumed importance of occupational factors as a determinant of psychological maladjustment is the fact that occupational therapy is usually the first treatment approach used in dealing with several varieties of mental illness. Such therapy attempts to provide patients with work activities that are both personally and socially meaningful.

Sociologically speaking, gainful employment, more than a simple matter of individual desire, is also largely a matter of social expectation. Taking note of this, one sociologist has pointed out that "a degree of self–respect derives from the fact that one works"[11] and that by working one has done something valued by society.

Consistent with the finding of such work–derived self–respect, a recent study determined that it varies according to the value placed by society on the particular job held. The study traced the careers of many workers. It found that job changes correlate high with changes in self–esteem, and that esteem is lower after job changes for workers initially high in self–esteem.[12]

In addition to the psychological effects of work, a person's job has implications for his social relations away from work. While on the job the worker learns and follows certain patterns of social interaction which are usually carried over after working hours. Attitudes and knowledge about human relations—relations with all people as well as with particular types—are acquired largely on the job through daily face–to–face contact and communication and much is learned both consciously and unconsciously about how to treat others and what treatment to expect in return. Additionally, many friendships which are continued after hours can form at work.

In one study, it was found that the way people are treated at work by both superiors and peers affects the way they treat others on the outside. The study reported that "the men who were bullied at work bullied their wives and their children in turn."[13]

Not only is the character of social relations away from the job influenced by on–the–job encounters, but the very extent of after–work relations can also be influenced by experiences at work. A recent work disclosed that the degree to which people participate in social groups in the community is largely determined by the way they are accepted by peer groups at work.[14] Even the kinds of people with whom one chooses to associate after hours appears to be job–related. For example, if young people encounter few persons outside their age group on the job, they will very likely shy away from social contact with older people off the job. In other words, personal prejudices can be influenced by experiences on the job.

An example of this is racial prejudice. All prejudices are either developed or reinforced through on–the–job experiences. It has been found that people who work in a racially mixed group are likely to have less prejudice and, consequently, be more inclined to engage in interracial relations after hours than workers in segregated work environments.

A recent situation brought this into focus. In 1963 Birmingham, Alabama, was torn by racial strife. As blacks and whites in the city became increasingly polarized and tension heightened, the only constructive help to relieve the situation seemed to be coming from the outside—from Federal officials and civil rights leaders. Feeling that Birmingham should do something itself about its crisis, outside leaders pointed to the fact that the United States Steel Company, the largest private employer in the city, was doing nothing to help, and that it could do something. They alleged that the large conglomerate over the years had actually contributed to the pattern of discrimination and the climate of racial disharmony that plagued Birmingham by its adoption of discriminatory and segregationist policies.

Following this accusation, a national campaign was launched to try to make United States Steel change its ways. The company finally did change and, many now feel, so has the community. United States Steel's reforms included opening up better jobs to blacks, permitting a racial mix beyond the

lowest rungs of the company's occupational ladder, and eliminating segregation in such facilities as washrooms and drinking
fountains.

A book that sought to show that racial contacts in industry
affect community race relations discusses how race relations
are influenced in developing countries when industrialization
introduces new occupations and new types of work organiza-
.tions. It concludes that industrialization by putting people with
different ethnic backgrounds at work on different phases of a
single operation makes them interdependent in getting the overall task done. Yet the book suggests the hypothesis that race
relations at work merely reflect race relations in society and,
thus, "changes in the racial order in industry are due to the
pressure of new situations that arise in the outside society?"[15]
But the facts indicate that this is not the case. For the fostering
of interracial contacts and racial equality in industry is often
an arbitrary matter having little relation to society's moral
standards or social values. For example, in the United States
business organizations which have adopted policies of integration and racial equality have not done so gradually or through
the careful weighing of moral considerations. Typically, the
new policies have been forced on them through governmental
actions, including fair employment legislation, court decisions,
and such administration measures as "equal opportunity" stipu-
lations in government contracts.

An example is the IBM operation in Poughkeepsie,
New York, which recently launched a campaign to recruit,
train, and place large numbers of black workers in all major
departmental operations. This move was not due to any community pressures on IBM but, rather, to the stipulation in
large Federal contracts. Yet the move is causing the community to become increasingly integrated since many newly hired
black employees are relocating to the area with their families.

In addition to interracial contacts in industry having a
bearing on community racial composition and race relations,
community class structure and social contacts between members of different social classes are influenced by industry. The

classic essays of Karl Marx make reference to this. Marx felt that the division of labor in the world of work shows up in the makeup of society. He pointed out that in premodern times, class consciousness among rich and poor alike was not very great. This, he said, was because large industrial organizations did not exist to bring people of the same class into close working contact with each other. Marx argued that as work organizations increased in size, people in similar employment situations began to identify closely with each other. In other words, they saw themselves as being in the same predicament, in the same class, so to speak, with similar interests and aspirations.

Adding support to Marx's work–oriented theory of class consciousness is the observation of contemporary sociologists that a person's occupation is an important criterion of his social desirability. Before a person who is unknown to a particular social group is allowed to become a member, his occupation, among other things, is usually learned and rated. In this way his acceptability is judged. Observing this, one American sociologist states: "Occupational role is one of the major bases of status in this nation; thus, the occupations which individuals hold in industry tend to confer certain amounts of status in the community."[16] And clearly, one's status in the community largely determines the potential limits of his social relations. An urban sociologist points out that people with similar occupations even join the same social activities. "Occupation itself," he states, "rather than a secondary trait, is the main basis of grouping. The potential number of categoric units (cliques, clubs, common interest associations, etc.) based directly upon occupations may be counted in the thousands."[17]

Thus far the concern of this chapter has been with how the social and psychological consequences of work help shape behavior away from the job. Another area in which work figures prominently as an influence on behavior is in its effect on the political behavior of people—their voting patterns, their political involvement, and their perspective on public issues.

Political scientists studying the political behavior of people have consistently taken employment experience and job situations into account in their analyses. A study in great depth found that people in different occupations tended to vote differently. Blue–collar workers were found to vote largely for the Democratic party and to take more liberal stands on public issues, while white–collar workers tended to vote Republican and to have basically conservative leanings. The study also found that not only is occupation an important determinant of political attitudes and behavior, but so are daily experiences on the job. Even within the same occupation (the printer's trade was used in the analysis) workers tended to think and act differently politically. These differences seemed to be related to such job factors as place of work, hours of work (the shift), and the nature of the job held. With few exceptions, people who worked at night or in small organizations were found to vote as their trade traditionally voted. The explanation given was that there is greater interaction among such workers and thus more opportunities for the political leanings of the occupation as a whole to be transmitted to and internalized by workers.[18]

Political apathy and extremism were the focus of another study that also took employment factors into consideration. Here the work backgrounds and on–the–job experiences of the people studied proved important. The conclusion was that people who experience frequent job changes or who are dissatisfied with their jobs tend to become apathetic or extremist in their political behavior.[19]

Another study found as an additional political consequence of one's work that "an important relationship exists between the status and power of an individual on his job and the status and power of his family."[20] A maintenance worker and his family, for example, are likely to have less power and political influence in a community than a corporation president and his family.

A final point regarding the implications of work for political behavior concerns the fact that workers sometimes vote according to the political preferences of their employers. Sometimes this is done out of an identification with the employer's best interests and the feeling that what is good for the employer is good for the people dependent upon him for their jobs. Other times employers successfully coerce their employees to follow a certain pattern of political behavior. This seems to be very common, as was brought out in a book by the present writer. The book reported that the power base of the politically dominant people in a community studied derived largely from the fact that they employed large numbers in the community and demanded their concurrence on community political issues.[21]

4

JOBS FOR THE UNSKILLED

A job placement specialist working with ghetto residents revealed in an interview that he was experiencing frustration. He was able to find jobs, but often could not find the people to take them, despite the fact that the unemployment rate in the area was over 20 percent. Rather than blame the people, he blamed the jobs. "Most young men on the streets," he explained, "refuse to do the crap jobs available."

The jobs to which he referred were menial, dead–end jobs. Professionals in the manpower field refer to these as unskilled, low–wage, low–skill or entry–level positions. They exist in large numbers in every industry and are the least meaningful, lowest paying, most "dead–end" jobs available. Minority members, deprived of educational and training opportunities available to others, traditionally have been allocated to these jobs. Today they are held predominantly by black workers.

Features of Unskilled Jobs

Faced with an acute labor shortage during World War I, U.S. industry looked for ways of supplementing its traditional labor supply. One particularly desperate factory owner undertook a daring experiment. He arranged with a mental institution to establish a hospital annex close to his plant and allow patients to take over assembly–line jobs in the factory during the day.

The first contingent of mental patients in the experiment were retarded women with an average mental age of 11 years old. After some time on the job, the reported results were unmistakable:

> They were fully, wholly and congenially employed. They were themselves extremely happy, and they rattled through their work with the dexterity of veterans. Not only their working companions, who labored under the apparent disadvantage of full mental stature, but also the managers were surprised at how efficient they were.[1]

This experience captures the essence of unskilled jobs. They involve simple, repetitive operations and little thought, judgment, or initiative. It can rightly be said that the innate intelligence that characterizes the human species seems to play no part in their performance. This intelligence can indeed be a handicap.

Among the 76 unskilled workers interviewed in the present study, more than twenty categories of unskilled positions were represented. Some job titles were dishwasher, kitchen helper, packer, file clerk, floorman, machine operator, assembler, shipping helper, laborer, and porter. Several workers' descriptions of their job duties follow:

¶ "I pull food carts to different floors and do odd jobs in the kitchen."

¶ "I run a dishwashing machine and take care of all cleaning chores."

¶ "I load an automatic stapler used on the assembly line."

¶ "I wait for orders for cardboard boxes and then deliver them to departments."

¶ "I clean and scrape dishes, rack them up, and send them through the dishwashing machine; then someone else takes them off at the other end."

¶ "I pick up an order from the office, get stock from shelves, pack the order, weigh it on a scale, and ship it."

¶ "I assemble part of a lighting fixture using an air wrench."

A number of characteristics of unskilled jobs deserve consideration. The most obvious is their demand for a maximum of physical and a minimum of mental effort. These jobs often tax the body to the point of fatigue at the same time as they underutilize the mind to the point of stagnation. Another feature of such jobs is that they provide few opportunities for individual accomplishment and self–expression. The tasks performed are highly segmentalized and give the worker contact with only a very small part of a large and complex operation. The work is also entirely preplanned and carefully supervised so that self-determination is all but impossible. In assembly work, the pace is controlled by the speed of a conveyor belt.

Karl Marx pointed out that with increasing division of labor, unskilled jobs become more and more simplified and, consequently, increasingly meaningless. In the process, Marx stated, the worker "becomes transformed into a simple monotonous force of production, with neither physical nor mental elasticity." Unskilled jobs are also highly unstable jobs. For their performance requires virtually no specialized training, only a small amount of on–the–job instruction. Thus workers can be easily replaced since any special talents they might have bear no relation to the job. "His work," observed Marx, "becomes accessible to all; therefore competitors press upon him from all sides."[2]

The insecurity inherent in these jobs increases as workers get older because they become less capable of enduring the physical demands. Additional insecurity results from the threat to unskilled jobs from machines. Each year tens of thousands of unskilled jobs are eliminated through mechanization and automation, a trend expected to continue in the future. It is expected that skilled and white–collar jobs will increase greatly, while lesser skilled positions will increase only slightly or decline.

TABLE 5
EMPLOYMENT BY OCCUPATION GROUP, 1970 AND 1980
(In Thousands)

	1970	Projected 1980
Professional and Technical Workers	11,140	15,500
Managers, Officials, and Proprietors	8,239	9,500
Clerical Workers	13,714	17,300
Sales Workers	4,854	6,000
Craftsmen and Foremen	10,158	12,200
Operatives	13,909	15,400
Service Uorkers	9,712	13,100
Nonfarm Laborers	3,724	3,500

Source: Manpower Report of the President, U.S. Department of Labor, 1972.

Another feature of unskilled jobs not to be overlooked is that they are typically very boring. They involve little imagination, creativity, or even change of pace. All they usually entail is a single, simple operation to be performed hour after hour, day after day. The frequent assumption that a worker eventually accustoms himself to and accepts their boring nature has been disclosed to be erroneous by a study which reported that over time a group of assembly–line workers were increasingly unhappy with the repetitive nature of their jobs and absolutely no adjustment occurred.[3]

Unskilled jobs often require work on night shifts. The problems imposed by not working a normal 9–to–5 day will be considered in a later discussion of the family life and social activities of unskilled workers.

A very important—though not necessarily the most important—characteristic of unskilled jobs, is the low wages paid. They are sometimes inadequate to meet normal living expenses and almost always inadequate to permit the accumulation of savings to meet emergencies. A recent study of poverty in the United States defined the poor to include "many of the employed—people employed at substandard wages."[4] A concise explanation of why unskilled jobs pay low wages was provided by Karl Marx:

It must be remembered that the more simple, the more easily learned the work is, so much the less is its cost of production, the expense of its acquisition, and so much the lower must the wages sink—for, like the price of any other commodity, they are determined by the cost of production. Therefore, in the same measure in which labor becomes more unsatisfactory, more repulsive, does competition increase and wages decrease.[5]

At a series of congressional hearings in 1968 termed "Employment and Manpower Problems in the Cities," it was revealed that despite the existence of a high unemployment rate, most blacks had jobs. Dr. Elliot Liebow of the National Institute of Mental Health therefore asked: "If most Negroes have jobs, what, then, is the problem?" He proceeded to answer his own question. "It is mainly that most of these jobs pay $50 to, say, $80 per week. The man with a wife and one or two children who takes such a job can be certain he will live in poverty so long as he keeps it. The longer he works, the longer he cannot live on what he makes."[6]

A later study of the economic characteristics and consequences of unskilled jobs concluded: "The problem is that even those who work—or a very large proportion of them—do not and cannot earn enough money to support their families. They work for a living but not for a living wage."[7]

Special surveys of 51 urban areas included in the 1970 Census revealed that 60 percent of all workers there did not earn enough for a decent standard of living for their families, while 30 percent could not even earn a poverty–level income.

A final point about unskilled jobs is that they are essentially "dead–end." They rarely serve as a stepping–stone to higher level jobs because the experience gained does not produce any useful employment skills. The fact that few promotions occur among unskilled workers was borne out in the present study. Only one out of five workers had ever received a promotion of any type, despite the fact that the majority were with their employer for many years. The frequency of promotions was only slightly greater in hospitals than in plants.

Considering some of the characteristics of unskilled jobs summarized above, the famous sociologist Eli Chinoy termed them "a form of daily imprisonment."[8]

Features of Unskilled Workers

U.S. Congressman Corman of California reflected on a trip he made to Mississippi: "I discovered Negroes were not permitted to drive garbage trucks. They could ride on the back and dump the garbage, but under the mores of 1963 in Jackson, Mississippi, they weren't qualified to drive the truck."[9]

This pattern of blacks confined occupationally at the bottom while whites may rise has been frequently observed, as well as documented in several formal studies. One U.S. Department of Labor study shows that blacks are relatively few in white–collar jobs but rather tend to be concentrated in blue–collar and service occupations. Another Department of Labor study examines the problem of poverty and estimates the number of poor families in this country. Its estimate is that of employed persons 35 percent of blacks and only 8 percent of whites are poor.[10]

TABLE 6
EMPLOYED PERSONS 16 YEARS AND OVER IN THE UNITED STATES, BY
OCCUPATION GROUP AND BY RACE (1971)

Occupation Group	Nonwhite	White
White-collar Workers	29.1%	50.6%
Blue-collar Workers	39.9%	33.7%
Service Workers	27.6%	11.8%
Other (Farm Managers and Laborers)	3.4%	3.9%
Total	100%	100%

Source: U.S. Department of Labor, *Manpower Report of the President,*
(April 1972), p. 173.

Another Department of Labor study reported on the progress that had been made by blacks in moving up to better jobs. It noted that despite six years of occupational advances, over two thirds of black male workers and three fifths of black female workers remained in service, laboring, or farm jobs. This, the study reported, was "substantially more than twice the proportion among whites."[11]

Regional studies of employment trends in various urban areas have arrived at similar conclusions. A survey conducted

in the Cleveland Metropolitan Area, for example, found that
blacks held only 3.2 percent of the white–collar jobs while
comprising 13 percent of the population.[12] A New York study
found that a fairly high percentage (5.7%) of blacks in the
area held white–collar jobs. But further investigation revealed
that "the vast majority of them (black white–collar workers)
are low paid clerical workers."[13] Further evidence of restricted
opportunities for blacks is the fact that their percentage in
the well–established professions is extremely low. In all, blacks
make up 3 percent of the physicians in this country, 3 percent
of the dentists, 2 percent of the engineers, 2 percent of the
business managers, 1 percent of the architects, and 1 percent of
the accountants and auditors.

Although black workers usually are not found in high
level positions, some areas of employment seem to offer more
opportunities than others. In public agencies, for example,
blacks comprise a relatively large proportion of white–collar
workers. Yet many private employers because of personal
prejudices do not employ blacks at all at the white–collar level.
There are still many companies, in fact, that do not employ
a single black in any position. Out of 4,249 New York City
firms that completed a mail survey questionnaire in the late
1960's, 27 percent said they did not employ a single black
in any capacity, while 43 percent had no black employees in
white–collar jobs.[14]

A study in Baltimore of the extent of minority group
representation in companies holding city government contracts
revealed that less than 1 percent had minority group employees
at all levels of management and labor. The firms reported
that 57.5 percent of minority personnel were employed as
semiskilled operators, unskilled laborers, and service workers.
Only 10.1 percent occupied managerial, professional, or technical jobs.[15]

A study in Cleveland reported on the number of "black
breakthroughs" in job categories previously held exclusively
by whites. Two types of "breakthroughs" were specified. "Primary breakthroughs" were defined as the hiring or promotion

of blacks into jobs not previously held by them in the greater Cleveland area. "Secondary breakthroughs" were the hiring or promotion of blacks into jobs they had not previously held in a particular plant or office. Primary and secondary breakthroughs for the year studied were 232. This impressive figure actually looked better on paper than it was in fact. As the report conceded, "the data overestimate the total number of actual job breakthroughs." For some of the primary breakthroughs consisted of only one black person attaining a job in a previously all white occupational category, something that could hardly be classified as an achievement of any great magnitude. A better word than breakthrough might have been "tokenism." Moreover many of the secondary breakthroughs occurred in companies where blacks had been kept not only in unskilled jobs, but in the lowest job category possible. One company where a breakthrough was reported had promoted a black worker for the first time to the job of truck driver.[16]

The pattern of black workers concentrated in bottom–level occupational categories is not restricted to a particular region of the country but is nationwide and is the same among both black males and females and regardless of educational level.

Data on the number of employed men and women in the country in different occupational categories show that in white–collar jobs white men outnumber black men proportionately by about three to one. The same threefold disparity between whites and blacks also exists among women. One difference is that although both black men and black women are concentrated in unskilled jobs, the men tend to work in industrial settings while the women are found more frequently in service occupations, including domestics in private households.[17]

One study argued there were somewhat better jobs for black women than for black men at low skill levels. The study pointed out that in 1960 the median income for black women was 93 percent of that for white women, while black men's median was only 68 percent of white men's.[18] These facts were used to explain why there were almost as many black women as black men employed, while among whites two and one–half times as many men as women worked.

As noted, educational attainment does not seem to influence the pattern of blacks being employed in jobs at lower levels than whites. Among white and nonwhite high school graduates between 16 and 24 years of age in the mid–1960's, a larger proportion of nonwhites were in jobs requiring little or no skill. Fifteen percent of the nonwhite graduates reported being employed as laborers, compared to 9.8 percent of the whites. Also 15.6 percent of the nonwhite graduates were employed as service workers in comparison to only 4.8 percent of the whites.[19]

TABLE 7
EMPLOYED NONWHITE AND WHITE HIGH SCHOOL GRADUATES
16-24 YEARS OLD, BY OCCUPATIONAL CATEGORY (1965)

Occupational Category	Nonwhite	White
Professional, technical, and kindred workers	6.8%	10.4%
Managers, officials, and proprietors, except farm	2.7%	6.4%
Clerical and kindred workers	8.2%	11.5%
Salesworkers	1.4%	7.1%
Craftsmen, foremen, and kindred workers	9.3%	14.4%
Operatives and kindred workers	37.8%	31.2%
Private household workers	—	.1%
Service workers, except private household	15.6%	4.8%
Farmers, farm managers, laborers and foremen	3.0%	4.3%
Laborers, except farm and mine	15.1%	9.8%
Total	100%	100%

Source: U.S. Department of Labor, *The Negroes in the United States,* (June 1966), p. 128.

When the incomes of blacks and whites are compared, with educational level kept constant, the pattern of inequality again emerges at each educational level. Vivian Henderson, President of Clark College, a black institution in Atlanta, commented: "The fact is that most Negroes have more education than they need for the kind of jobs they can get."[20]

Workers employed in unskilled jobs, whether black or white, tend to live in lower quality communities by virtue of their low wages. The unskilled black worker, whose meager wages usually are not enough to raise his family above the poverty level, will almost always be found living in an impoverished ghetto community. Even when the income is higher than the poverty mark, it is rarely adequate to allow escape from the ghetto.

A national survey of three million poor families with male heads under 65 years old found that half of the male household workers had full–time, year–round jobs. They were simply low–paid, unskilled workers—the working poor.[21]

The unskilled black workers and a substantial majority of the paraprofessionals interviewed in the present study lived in ghetto areas. Even the paraprofessionals' average salary of about $110 per week was insufficient to leave their slum communities. Our survey also found that relatively few unskilled workers owned their own home and that only slightly more of the paraprofessionals were homeowners. In all, 85.5 percent of the unskilled workers were renters compared to 81.2 percent of the paraprofessional workers. Another feature of the unskilled workers in our survey was that fully 10 percent of them had their previous residence in the South.

In concluding this discussion of the characteristics of unskilled workers, background profiles of some who were interviewed will be presented. One worker, a 32–year–old father of three with a fourth child on the way, was born and raised on a farm in Lawrenceville, Virginia. He moved to Baltimore when he married at the age of 26. He had graduated from a vocational high school, where he completed a course in auto mechanics. But he found it impossible to get work in the area of his training and worked as a general laborer in a stone quarry before obtaining his present position in a hospital cafeteria.

Another worker, a 40–year–old Baltimore native, has worked in the hospital that employs her for twelve years. She started at 85 cents per hour and now earns $1.79 as a pantry aide. Previously she was employed in another hospital as a laundry and linen sorter. Before, she worked as an occasional domestic.

A middle–aged divorcee working in a meat processing

plant was born in New Orleans, where she was orphaned at
an early age. She studied history and English at a college in
the South but dropped out. She thinks of going back to school
to finish her education, but admitted that she would probably
have to stick to her factory job in order to support her children.

A 34–year–old bachelor who came to the North four
years ago was found working at an unskilled job in a hospital.
He was born and educated in Richmond, Virginia, and upon
completing high school attended a trade school for a year and
a half and learned tailoring. He has never used the training
but began working at the hospital as a kitchen helper four
years ago, and today he is still a kitchen worker.

Why Blacks Are at the Bottom

There is little doubt widespread racial discrimination,
both past and present, is the foremost reason why black workers are concentrated in unskilled jobs. The other factors are
relatively minor in comparison. In the remainder of this chapter the specific discriminatory practices of industry that have
played a direct role in keeping black workers at the bottom
will be noted, while Chapter 5 will consider in detail the many
other types of exclusion and exploitation that blacks have
historically experienced in the United States.

At a hearing in 1968 on discrimination in white–collar
employment, the United States Equal Employment Opportunity Commission disclosed that nearly 50 percent of the com-
plaints about discrimination it had received were filed by employed persons who felt they had been discriminated against
in promotional opportunities. Thus, much of the discrimination in employment was found to exist not in initial hiring but
in advancement opportunities.

The discrimination in hiring people to fill positions other
than entry–level jobs is often accomplished through carefully
conceived and cleverly disguised means. The hearing revealed
the frequency with which employment agencies accept dis-

criminatory job orders from employers who simply do not want to hire a black worker for other than an entry–level position.

Recent laws that bar discrimination in hiring are very difficult to enforce, particularly among small employers. It is the small organization that hires friends and relatives, or people of the same background, and where the personal prejudices of the boss can come into play.

Discrimination in promotions is most responsible for the alarmingly low percentage of blacks in other than entry–level positions. This discrimination persists not only in the face of prohibitory laws but also despite the official policy of many companies. An incident was reported of a foreman in an electronics plant who recommended that a young black janitor be promoted to the job of wirer/starter on the production line. The factory superintendent reacted by calling the foreman into his office and telling him, "You just can't do this. It would start a hornet's nest in your department." But the foreman pointed out that the company had a nondiscriminatory policy. "Then you'd better take your recommendation to the president," the superintendent answered, "because he's the one who made the policy."[22]

Even some companies with nondiscrimination policies apply them differently in various branch operations to reflect the community norms. It is not uncommon, for example, for large corporations to follow one course of action in the South and a different one in the North. The President of Western Union admitted that although his company had long employed minority people, such employment was limited largely to "nonquality" jobs, with only a scattering of blacks in clerical and lower management positions. At the time he made this disclosure in 1968, he noted that nonwhites were beginning to be used as telegraph operators, telephone operators, and technicians in the large Northern cities. But he admitted that during his stay with the company, "like so many other companies our employment patterns and practices were determined by local customs instead of uniformly enforced company policy."[23]

It is hardly necessary to point out that in the many parts

of the United States where the appearance of a black face in a high–level job is very rare indeed political and community pressure is exerted on newly arrived companies to maintain the *status quo*. They are expected to help preserve the prevailing social system, not serve as a catalyst to alter it. Robert Weaver, former Secretary of Housing and Urban Development, pointed out: "There is less opposition to Negroes doing hot, heavy, dirty and lower paid work than clean, light and higher paid work. This is in accordance with the concept of color–caste system since the former type of employment is obviously more in keeping with the status of a people stigmatized as inferior."[24]

The discrimination against blacks exists uniformly—it does not appear to be influenced much by such factors as sex, age, or level of education. When it comes to promotions, however, the older black worker and the female black worker are faced with double discrimination since preference for promotion is usually given to young, male workers. As far as education is concerned, the uneducated black person will probably have somewhat more difficulty in obtaining a promotion than if he was educated. But as data previously cited showed, the confinement of blacks to low occupational categories cuts across educational levels. One manpower expert took note of this and commented on the choices that a black youth has when considering whether to obtain an education. "He can forget about getting an education and become a busboy or a janitor who cannot read or write, or he can work hard at getting an education and become a busboy or a janitor who can read and write. In either event, if he becomes a busboy or a janitor and works hard, he becomes—after a few years—a hard–working busboy or janitor."[25]

There is little question that a great deal of the discrimination against blacks is not due to any quasipractical questions of talent or ability but merely to blind bigotry. They are simply not wanted around. The reasoning of a bigot is typified in a board meeting of a major Chicago bank about twenty years ago when a member suggested that some blacks be hired.

The board chairman, shocked by the suggestion, lead the vote to defeat the proposal after pointing out the board members would be sitting on the same toilet seats as the blacks.[26]

Sometimes discrimination against blacks takes place in the absence of overt bigotry. Management personnel in selecting workers for promotions often choose those with backgrounds and characteristics most like themselves. This is done ostensibly for purposes of compatibility, and the demand for compatibility seems to increase at higher job levels. According to one management expert, "likemindedness" within a working group has some real advantages, including the suppositions that "communication is quick and easy" and that "members feel comfortable and secure with one another."[27]

An added problem is that discrimination away from the job contributes to keeping the black worker on the lower end of the occupational ladder. Housing discrimination is one example. A promotion in a large company often involves moving to a new community. Several companies have experienced difficulty persuading black employees to move to cities in the South, even when desirable homes could be secured for them. Many simply do not want to move into entirely segregated neighborhoods or go into a region where they would clearly have second–class citizen status.

Another factor that limits promotional opportunities for blacks is prejudice on the part of white peers at work. The prejudice is often so intense that a newly appointed black supervisor cannot function in his position. Many companies have found that because of peer prejuduce, when they promote a black worker to supervisor, they "lose a good producer and gain an ineffectual manager."[28]

Many blacks occupy entry–level positions because they are recent migrants from the South. A study called this migrant population "the uprooted" and found many difficulties facing them in adapting to the needs of a modern industrial labor force. It noted: "Their few salable skills, their lack of formal education, their commitment to agrarian values, indeed, their initial gullibility, place them in positions where they may be exploited by employers."[29]

A final reason that can be offered to explain why there are relatively few blacks in other than entry–level jobs is because of the methods available to find good jobs. People often rely upon the information and influence of friends and relatives to obtain jobs. A study found: "the most common method is recommendation by a friend or relative, usually one working for the same employer; relatively few people find jobs through newspaper advertisements and even fewer through government or private employment agencies."[30] Since few blacks have relatives or friends working for corporations in any position but a lower–level job, they are clearly at a disadvantage when it comes to job hunting.

5

EXCLUSION AND EXPLOITATION: THE BLACK HERITAGE

The history of the black American is a bleak, dismal, and rather distressing story. It is a history of exclusion and exploitation, of poverty and discrimination. It is also a history with few highs or lows. The black man's condition has been consistently below that of whites—in war and peace, in depression and prosperity. Unlike the immigrants who experienced a drop in status upon arriving in America and who then later rose up, the black man started out low and has stayed low. He has indeed moved around—from rural areas to urban areas, from cotton fields to factories, from slavery to non-slavery—but his condition has remained rather constant. The history of American blacks is highly instructive, for it helps in understanding the black man's situation today.

Black Americans comprise a unique group, a group whose experiences, values, and traditions are unlike any other. In the words of James Baldwin, "the American Negro is a unique creation; he has no counterpart anywhere, and no predecessors."[1]

The Slave Tradition

James Baldwin has described black American history as a history of "rope, fire, torture, castration, infanticide, rape; death and humiliation; fear by day and night, fear as deep as the marrow of the bone; doubt that he was worthy of life, since everyone around him denied it."

The main themes running through black American history are slavery, exploitation, and rejection. This background includes a good deal of work experience, but work that was done under the most intolerable and inhuman of conditions. It is not a work background to look to proudly, and few blacks do so. The "Uncle Tom" image of the placid slave working contentedly in the fields is held today by many whites, but by few blacks. They know better. There are still a few former living slaves, while in many black families memories of the slave period are kept alive, passed down by word–of–mouth from generation to generation. A black author dedicated a book to a relative living in the "Uncle Tom" era as follows: "To my Uncle George Woodson who in captivity in America manifested the African spirit of resistance to slavery and died fighting the institution."[2]

Most blacks today realize that their family name is not of African origin and in no way reflects their ancestry. It is a name that was bestowed by a slave owner to identify his property, in the same manner as the ranch owner who brands his cattle. On this James Baldwin has commented:

It is a fact that every American Negro bears a name that originally belonged to the white man whose chattel he was. I am called Baldwin because I was either sold by my African tribe or kidnapped out of it into the hands of a white Christian named Baldwin, who forced me to kneel at the foot of the cross. I am, then, both visibly and legally the descendant of slaves in a white, Protestant country, and this is what it means to be an American Negro, this is who he is—a kidnapped pagan, who was sold like an animal and treated like one, who was once defined by the American Constitution as "three-fifths" of a man, and who, according to the Dred Scott decision, had no right that a white man was bound to respect.[3]

While white workers share the "Protestant ethic"—a heritage of free labor and independence in the world of work —black workers have only the slave ethic. The Protestant ethic, it is claimed, gives those who share it a "puritanical devotion to work for work's sake."[4] Thus, most whites, even lower–level job holders, often feel compelled to work and to find some enjoyment in it, frequently claiming, "It is a natural thing to enjoy work." But the slave tradition of blacks produces an ethic that makes it very difficult to accept work, particularly the type offered by unskilled jobs since this work has many of the characteristics of slave labor.

Another factor having a bearing on the black man's situation today that can also be traced to the slave experience is the high degree of frequency of broken families. Persistence of the pattern is encouraged by adverse economic conditions and a public welfare system in which broken families often fare best.

The immigrants who came to this country (from the Pilgrims to the Puerto Ricans) relied heavily on the family unit as a source of strength in their fight for survival. But the slaves, though they too sought to develop and maintain strong families, were effectively prevented from doing so. Their masters periodically, and permanently, separated family members to keep families from surviving for any extended period. The slaveholders had two reasons for doing this. First, they placed a premium on unfettered reproduction, which could only be achieved by systematically maintaining promiscuity among their slaves. Secondly, they wanted to keep the slaves from easily uniting in rebellion.[5] The slaveholders recognized that family dissolution would make it more unlikely for larger coalitions to form. Broken families have thus helped keep blacks powerless and contributed to the hopelessness and despair often prevalent in the ghetto.

Another black tradition intensifying dissatisfaction with unskilled work that had its origin in the slavery period is nonaggressiveness, as reported by two black psychiatrists. Aggressive slaves were considered a threat to the system and were killed. Nonaggressiveness was therefore valued as a means of survival. It continues to be valued today, these authors argue, largely through the influence of fearful black women. They firmly believe that whites are still in complete control and are merely accommodating blacks. If a black person is too forward, they feel he will upset this delicate situation and tip the balance against him.[6]

The fear that some blacks have of being aggressive, of taking the initiative both in the community and on the job, is based on more than tradition. It is due, to some degree, on day–to–day experiences. Unlike the slave of the past, the black ghetto resident today is not killed when he displeases whites. But he can be, and often is, severely punished.

The black worker who questions, criticizes, or otherwise defies his white supervisor is often fired on the spot. And in the community, the recalcitrant black person may have his relief check taken away or have a son on probation remanded back to jail. The timidity that blacks inherited from the slave period is thus kept alive through contemporary experiences.

In the work setting, this nonaggressive tradition can amplify job discontentment. For unlike white workers who feel comfortable in being aggressive in attempting to improve their occupational situation, the black man is often wary.

The black norm of nonaggressiveness is actually reinforced on the job, as elsewhere, because blacks have learned that their efforts, even when equal to whites', will not bring comparable rewards. As one study of black and white workers found, black workers are far more fatalistic and feel they can do little on the job to improve their work situation.[7]

Prejudice and Discrimination

Racial discrimination can be found in America in many forms. In the community, it occurs in housing, education, and other important areas. At work, everything from peer treatment to management policies is often discriminatory. Exclusion from unions because of color has also been common.[8] This traditional unequal treatment has resulted in a low economic and political status. Commenting specifically on the black man's relative political impotency, James Baldwin has said: "Color is not a human or a personal reality; it is a political reality."[9]

There is little question that separate education makes blacks educationally inferior—regardless of whether the education they receive is really inferior. And poorly educated people lack the knowledge and skills needed to assume a meaningful role in society and tend not to have the motivation needed to improve their condition. Studies of motivation among blacks in segregated schools show that the greater the percentage of black students in the school, the lower their aspiration level. The findings are similar in both Northern and Southern schools.

In addition to being denied educational and other self–help opportunities, black Americans traditionally have been excluded from most important positions in society. This has had a number of serious consequences. It has meant that there have been few success models to which black youngsters could look to emulate or to be convinced that success was possible for them. The absence of such success models has contributed to apathy and feelings of hopelessness. Efforts to succeed are often viewed as a fruitless expenditure of energy.

Besides stifling motivation, there is an equally damaging consequence of the disproportionately small number of blacks in high–level positions. It is difficult for blacks to acquire the experience needed to operate effectively in such roles in business and political life either by firsthand experience or by observing or asking other blacks, since so few have been in these positions. Studies comparing black Americans to black West Indians in America have brought out this point. The West Indians are often found to be superior in business enterprise and educational achievement. This is attributed to the fact that they come from islands that are almost completely black and where blacks consequently hold most of the important positions.

Apathy and desperation are common attitudes among black ghetto residents. One community organizer, reflecting on his experiences, commented: "Every community consultant is familiar with the phenomenon of apathy, lack of response to his best efforts."[10] There is often a lack of motivation to try to improve conditions. When middle– and upper–class people with fair or ample resources fail in something, it will probably cost them only a small part of what they have. They are in a position to sustain short–term costs in an effort to achieve long–term goals and simply chalk the loss up to experience and proceed to the next item for their involvement. By contrast, the fear among black ghetto residents of losing the little they have is an important reason why they do not become more active. They are afraid that if they oppose an urban renewal proposal they will be denied relocation help, afraid that if they speak out against the welfare system they will be denied their check.

In the field of employment, besides confining blacks to low occupational levels, other types of discrimination are widespread in the South despite their prohibition by the Civil Rights Act of 1964. Many companies, for example, maintain separate lockers, toilets, cafeterias, vending machines, drinking fountains, and even time clocks for white and black employees. Two annual company picnics are given by many companies, one for black and the other for white workers. Even athletic teams are often formed along color lines. Moreover, throughout the country a large number of labor unions maintain discriminatory practices, although the official policy of the AFL–CIO is one of nondiscrimination. This is especially true of the more skilled trades, such as construction and railroad work, where there is strong union member opposition to the equal participation of blacks. It has been stated that trade unions "such as the international brotherhood of electrical workers, the plumbers union, the carpenters unions, and sheet metal workers international association, have an unfavorable record of discrimination and sometimes almost total exclusion from apprenticeships."[11] The New York State Commission for Human Rights announced in a 1964 decision that it had found the Sheet Metal Workers International Association, Local 27, guilty of having systematically barred blacks from membership throughout its seventy–six–year history. Not one of its more than 3,000 members was black at the time of the ruling.

One common error is the belief that discrimination against blacks takes place mostly against the young and un-educated and that mature blacks on the same educational level with whites encounter relatively little discrimination. In fact, one study found: "Discrimination is greatest against older and better–educated non–whites."[12] Relatively few blacks are given the opportunity to train for high–level professions or, if they do complete such training, to practice freely in their field. Statistics on the race of professionals show very few practicing black engineers, dentists, physicians, lawyers, and judges in the United States. This situation is particularly marked in the legal field. If a distaste for discrimination is postulated, the difference in numbers of the professions be-comes relevant; one factor is that lawyers must argue in white courts.[13]

It is often erroneously assumed that the greater the number of blacks in a particular profession, the less is the dis-crimination against them. "Discrimination against Negroes," notes one authority to the contrary, "seems to be positively correlated with their relative number."[14] This indicates that often a few blacks are accepted as a form of tokenism. When the number increases, whites who have harbored prejudice all along may become openly hostile.

Blacks encounter discrimination not only from employers and unions, but also in educational institutions. Thus, the black job applicant who is denied a position because an employer or union considers him inadequately trained may have already been the victim of educational discrimination. The phenom-enon of "separate but equal public schools" is still widespread in the United States today because of segregated residential areas.

Discrimination is also frequently found in job training programs. A plant in the deep South needed workers who could read at a certain grade level. Since the only workers available in the area were not qualified, the company developed a training program to bring its lower–level employees to the required level. A report on what happened follows: "In prospect were a number of jobs that would call for the reading of rudimentary reading instructions and making mathematical calculations. . . . Employees were notified that voluntary classes would be held to prepare them for promotion. The local school board agreed to cooperate, provided the classes were segregated."[15]

Numerous other forms of discrimination face blacks, despite a battery of prohibitory laws. The most comprehensive form of discrimination is residential segregation. There are very few integrated neighborhoods in the United States— they are either all white or all black. A government survey published in 1967 found that residential discrimination in eight of twelve cities studied was higher than in previous years. An equally distressing fact uncovered was that conditions in the black neighborhoods were "stagnant or deteriorating."[16]

The prevalence of race discrimination off the job reinforces the feelings of black workers that they are being treated unfairly at work. They are inclined to explain their confinement to a menial job in terms of the extensive discrimination that they have long known and not to any fault of their own.

The feeling of most blacks that they are second–class citizens results not merely from unequal opportunities but also from the many specific instances of prejudice and discrimination experienced on a day–to–day basis. This is illustrated in Dick Gregory's *Nigger,* a book about various situations in which he found himself. Once when he was a star athlete, a small crippled boy and his father approached him as he was walking down the street.

The little boy smiled, very shyly, and pulled out a ten-cent-store album. "Would you sign my autograph book?"

"Sure, John. Got a pencil?"

John didn't have a pencil. Neither did his father. It was a Sunday, and the only place we could get a pencil was the restaurant we were standing in front of. I turned to the father.

"They'll give you a pencil in there."

He looked at me a little strangely, but he went in and got a pencil. He handed it to me as if he thought I should have walked into the restaurant and gotten the pencil myself. I signed the autograph book, told John I'd be looking for him in the stands next week, and walked away quickly. I could feel the father's eyes on my back, could hear him thinking about some uppity nigger making him go fetch a pencil. Somehow I didn't feel I could explain to him that Negroes weren't allowed in that restaurant, that before I could have asked for a pencil I would have heard that woman behind the cash register say, "I'm sorry, but you know we're not allowed to serve colored in here . . ." I should have gotten that little crippled kid's autograph. He was an American.[17]

At the same time that whites treat blacks differently because of their color, blacks are themselves becoming increasingly color conscious. This has enabled them to become more aware of their situation as a group. They observe that in the organizations where they work the lowest jobs are held predominantly by blacks, while the skilled, supervisory, and executive positions are dominated by whites. And after work they return to their all–black, problem–plagued communities, often passing through the far better neighborhoods of whites. They see, as the late Martin Luther King pointed out, that they live with other blacks on "an island of poverty in a sea of white prosperity."[18]

It does not take much insight for blacks to know that the pattern of separation found both on and off the job is not the product of chance but largely of design. And their feelings of hopelessness, frustration, and deprivation are intensified by this knowledge. As noted by one authority, "the resulting relative deprivation is the fundamental basis of mass Negro–American dissatisfaction today."[19]

Recent Trends in America

American society has changed dramatically since the beginning of this century when the mass influx of immigrants occurred. Developments have taken place in all major fields —politics, economics, social affairs, and technology. Many of the changes have made it difficult for blacks to gain a firm footing in this country.

In the structure and functioning of government there has been a major trend toward centralization and control on the national level. The Federal government has assumed an increasingly dominant role in initiating, funding, and even in implementing programs for local areas. All major responsibilities of local government are today influenced in some significant way by the Federal government.

The shifting of many responsibilities from municipalities to the national government has made it increasingly difficult for people to influence policies. In the ghetto, where government plays an important role in servicing and supporting people, residents are little able to inform, much less influence, Washington officials as to their needs and desires. The ghetto resident feels that government officials are not really concerned about him and his problems. A scholar discussing the lack of participation of the poor in the talks surrounding the formulation of the Economic Opportunity Act noted: "The poor are not only cut off and excluded from most of this public conversation, but have little confidence in society's intentions toward them."[20]

A recent article by this writer on citizen participation among ghetto residents considered a variety of publicly and privately initiated programs to encourage greater participation. The conclusion was that most of these efforts are ill-conceived and often hamper meaningful participation. Some purportedly successful programs have increased participation at the expense of effective action. For example, one project aimed at improving conditions in a poverty area incorporated so many citizen committees to approve each step that little improvement was ever accomplished.[21]

In addition to the takeover by the Federal government of traditionally local functions, there have been changes in local government that have served to make ghetto residents feel detached from public policy. City governments have been growing larger, more complex, and more bureaucratic. This has caused many ghetto residents to feel ineffective in dealing with city government. Others are simply confused. In either case the result is the same. Ghetto residents, by and large, do not seek to become involved in governmental policy.

An article about welfare clients and public welfare departments maintained that people in the "lower strata" have little understanding of bureaucratic procedures and often regard service systems as structured deliberately to intimidate them. A conclusion was that "lack of motivation, anomie, alienation, and apathy can be traced to the duration and nature of involvement with the Department of Welfare" and that the "unmotivated" ghetto resident may in fact have been "demotivated."[22]

The General Revenue Sharing Act of 1972 was aimed at easing Federal control over local government. Henceforth local government could use Federal funds with minimum Federal supervision. This new arrangement was to give greater responsibility to local officials, cut down on red tape, and save money. It is regrettable that no provision was made for citizen participation, particularly if local officials follow the path they have chosen in the past—to disregard the needs and desires of the poor and politically powerless in setting priorities for spending public money.

An important economic trend that has worsened the economic situation of blacks is the general increase in the size of businesses, particularly nonservice businesses. With sharpened competition, the larger size of a business, the greater is its likelihood of survival. This new kind of economics places business ownership all but out of reach of the poor, for it is virtually impossible for them to acquire the substantial capital and management experience needed.

The trend to increasing unionization of labor often prevents blacks from even becoming workers. At the turn of the century when most workers and shops were not unionized, a job seeker merely had to acquire the skills needed, if any, and then approach an employer. Today, for many types of work, union membership is needed to get the job.

Labor unions, by definition, are concerned with the protection of their members. If current members can handle the work available, there is no need to admit new members, regardless of the employment demands of outsiders. When new members are admitted, the existing membership is considered to have the right to choose them. If they wish to help family members and friends by allowing them to join while excluding others, this is considered to be their prerogative. Pointing out the implications of this situation for the employment of blacks, one observer has commented: "A basic conflict exists between labor–union concepts and civil–rights concepts."[23] The additional barrier for blacks of racial discrimination exists in many unions as an unwritten, but firm, policy.

The increasingly important role of credit as against money in the United States economy is another trend that has proved harmful to blacks. People who are well off economically find it easier than the poor to obtain credit—credit to go to college, to start a business, to buy a car for traveling to work, and to do other things that could have long–term benefits.

The new credit economy has also opened up many new avenues for the exploitation of blacks. Ghetto businesses and door–to–door salesmen are notorious for their easy credit come–ons. The exorbitant rates of interest for often exorbitantly priced merchandise are often cleverly disguised. Nor is the buyer made to realize that not only can his possessions be impounded for missing a single payment, but his future earnings can legally be confiscated as well.

Another trend that has had ill effects for black ghetto

residents is the emergence of social organizations of ever–increasing size. This trend is a response to the increase in sheer numbers of people and to the general increase in the size and complexity of institutions. In order to be effective, people joining together in groups must also form large units. But large–scale organizations have been difficult for black ghetto residents either to create or join. It has been found that "people who lack skills have a low sense of personal efficacy in organizational situations."[24] In addition to their reluctance to join existing organizations, ghetto residents have faced obstacles in establishing organizations of their own. A major reason is that ghettos are characterized by unstable populations. Even in older ghettos where in–migration has ceased, stability is often disrupted. Governmental redevelopment projects such as urban renewal effectively serve to disrupt the community and to disperse its residents. When this happens, community organizations often disappear.

Many technological changes have had a direct bearing on the situation of ghetto blacks. Some major developments have occurred in industrial technology. The automation and mechanization widely applied in industry have eliminated many jobs. Not all of these jobs have been unskilled positions. Some were semiskilled jobs, jobs which at the beginning of the century provided immigrants with a means to learn a skill. The entry–level jobs that exist today are usually very basic because the high degree of mechanization demands that work operations be highly segmentalized. It is not rare to find workers today doing a very specific operation and not knowing what the end product is on which they are working.

Other developments have occurred in transportation technology. It is far easier and quicker today for people to travel short distances than it was 50 years ago. The development in transportation that has had greatest impact is the automobile. But improvements in transportation have had several results which have hindered the ghetto poor. For one thing, improved transportation has made the suburbs possible. It has also made it feasible for industries to locate in isolated sections away from their market areas. The suburbs have been a favorite relocation spot for affluent city residents. This has caused financial problems for cities, which have made it increasingly difficult to provide quality services to the poor who must remain. The movement of industry out of the city, meanwhile, has reduced the number of jobs available to city residents who do not have the money for an automobile.

Living in the Ghetto

It is a fact that most blacks live in communities that are far lower in quality than the communities of whites. It was earlier pointed out that unskilled workers are likely to seek the satisfaction after work hours that they are deprived on their jobs. But for black workers who must return after work to an overcrowded, impoverished, problem–plagued community, such satisfaction is hardly possible. Because of this, their menial jobs are that much more intolerable, their ill consequences that much more severe.

This holds true especially for night workers, and night shifts are common for holders of unskilled jobs. Adjustment to a night–work routine is difficult for all workers, but it is particularly difficult for the black worker who must seek rest during the day in a neighborhood characterized by "over–crowdedness, non–privacy, and noisy streets."[25]

Another ghetto feature that also serves to intensify dissatisfaction with unskilled jobs is that the ghetto as a community is usually not under the control of its residents. It has been pointed out that, "communities of the poor are controlled largely by the police or organized crime groups. . . ." Thus, the feeling of powerlessness that is produced by a menial job is reinforced for blacks in the community.

With physical and social conditions as they are in the ghetto, little compensation is available here for the ill effects of menial work. At the same time, the job can intensify dissatisfaction with the ghetto community. This occurs when a worker's place of employment is clean and neat, such as a hospital that provides a striking contrast to his living conditions. "Men working in clean and tidy factories," a recent study found, "demand also a higher standard at home."[27]

Intergenerational Mobility of Blacks

Leaving the community and home environment of blacks, a final characteristic of this population segment is worthy of mention, namely its small degree of intergenerational mobility. Statistics show that the occupational level of an unskilled black worker is likely to be no higher than his father's and his son's no higher than his.

Intergenerational mobility is actually very low among all lower–level workers, both white and black. A sociologist notes: "There is a strong tendency for the children of white–collar workers to inherit their father's occupational level or to climb above it, whereas children of manual workers tend to inherit their father's occupational level or fall below it."[28] For black workers, the probability that they have risen above their father's job level or that their children will rise above theirs is considerably lower than for white workers. One study found that blacks showed very little long–term mobility as a group. "As compared to the white workers," the study concluded, "Negroes occupy the lower occupational levels and have considerably less chance for rising."[29]

Most blacks realize that their condition as a group has remained relatively constant over the years. To point out that there have been certain advances in the economic level of blacks and a few breakthroughs in some areas of employment does not alter this fact. For blacks quite logically look at their condition relative to that of whites. "The average occupational position of Negroes," it has been noted, "has risen quite strikingly both in the North and South, but their position relative to whites has been remarkably stable. . . . Neither striking increases nor striking decreases in discrimination against

Negroes have occurred during the last four decades."[30] And the fact that blacks have achieved some advances has made little impression on them. "A man's lively sense of his own impoverishment and denial," it has been written, "must be measured chiefly in terms of what he perceives in relation to things that are close at hand."[31] The black man sees himself in a situation where he is "given the salad while whitey eats the turkey."[32] Though both the salad and the turkey have improved over the years, the difference between the two is as real as ever.

What does this mean to the unskilled black worker and how does it influence his reaction to his job? It was earlier pointed out that all workers are socially compelled to try to better themselves in America, but that lower–level workers are frustrated in this because they have limited opportunities for either personal satisfaction or occupational advancement. But many white low–level workers, particularly those with a recent immigrant background, can point to the fact that they have advanced beyond the job level of their father and, more importantly, they can realistically expect that their children will advance beyond them. But because little intergenerational mobility takes place among blacks, black workers usually cannot point to their fathers in this way nor expect that their sons will rise above them.

These and other factors make the black worker a special case among holders of unskilled jobs. His history and his present situation in American society serve to aggravate the ill consequences of menial work. More than his white peers, the feelings of hopelessness, powerlessness, deprivation, and despair produced by a menial, dead–end job are more intense for him. He is likely to believe, reflecting on his history, that "he has been robbed of his dignity, first by the slave system and later by the exploitative economy."[33] The following statement by a contemporary social critic laments the absence of a sufficient number of decent jobs for blacks:

> For the Negro man, unemployment, underemployment, and equally important, employment that is demeaning by its very

nature, all serve to compound injuries that society and his own family have inflicted on him from birth. The difficulty Negro men experience in finding a decent job—jobs that would accord them a measure of dignity and self-respect and permit them to play the male role of breadwinner—is essential to perpetuation of the matriarchy and of the weakness of family relationships.[34]

Despite the fact that throughout the history of America blacks have occupied second–class status and have had few opportunities either to shape their own destinies or influence the destiny of others, most blacks see the hard work they have performed in this country over the last 300 years as having helped make the United States what it is today, and they therefore feel they are entitled to a better deal than they are now receiving. In the words of one angry black man after giving the matter some thought, "Us Negroes helped build this fucking country, its ours as much as the ofays and we got a right to enjoy some of its comforts. By God we going to."[35]

6

BLACK WORKERS IN MENIAL JOBS

Emotional Problems and Unskilled Jobs

A study considering jobs of different levels in terms of their psychological implications for those who perform them observed:

> To the typical man in a middle-class occupation, working means having a purpose, gaining a sense of accomplishment, expressing himself. . . . To the typical man in a working-class occupation working means having something to do.[1]

Thus, the study argued that low–level jobs make less of a contribution to personal adjustment than higher level jobs.

Many studies of mental illness have pointed out that a person's job can have a positive or negative influence on his psychological stability. One study listed the following five traits of mentally healthy persons:

1. They have a wide variety of sources of gratification.
2. They are more flexible under stress.
3. They treat others as individuals.
4. They recognize, understand, and accept their own capacities and limitations.
5. They are active and productive.

The study determined that work involving routine tasks and limited responsibilities offers little opportunity for developing these healthy characteristics. It found that menial jobs hardly permit recognizing one's limitations, for example, because they present no challenge that would enable one to learn about himself and his true capabilities.[2]

Other commentators have developed similar themes. One finds that basic human needs include activity, sharing thoughts and feelings, and engaging in self–determination; each of these, he argues, is unfulfilled by menial jobs.[3] An industrial psychologist arrived at the conclusion that low–skill jobs are not conducive to optimal mental health.[4] A prominent social philosopher claimed that the less meaningful the work, the more difficult is a person's psychological adjustment to life.[5]

The Making of a Moron, discussed in Chapter 1, contains many insights into the ill effects menial, repetitive work has on psychological well–being, particularly when long continued. It points out that psychological adjustment occurs best in situations where individual decisions are allowed and that there is an inverse relationship between work specialization and worker satisfaction. Unskilled jobs are characterized both by few worker decisions and a high degree of specialization.

The dead–end nature of unskilled jobs has been found by many to have a strong negative influence on psychological well–being. Thus, it is reported that people with dead–end jobs "feel degraded and become demoralized."[6] Obtaining a better job—the way most Americans meet the strong social expectations to better themselves— is an avenue all but closed to menial job holders.

A major psychological function of work is its role in developing self–respect. One way a person can gain self–respect on the job is to win the approval of others. But a menial job provides little opportunity to demonstrate any talents that would gain the recognition of others. The tasks involved are usually so basic and clear–cut that one does them either right or wrong, not better or worse. Furthermore, the work requires no special skills. Even a stranger to it could do it satisfactorily with only basic instruction.

Self–respect also derives from jobs that are not so routine or mechanical that a machine could easily do them. But many unskilled jobs can be, and indeed often are, taken over by machines. An unskilled worker who had been employed in different companies described the situation in the storage and shipping company where he currently worked. He related that the morale was high there, unlike other places where he worked, because few machines were used and many tasks could only be done by human mind and muscle. The workers' morale was also furthered by opportunities to vie with one another in exhibitions of strength. Noting such daily contests, the worker remarked: "Childish? Perhaps more accurately childlike. They did not have much to be proud of but they had something and that is the beginning of self–respect."[7] In addition, in this company each worker could see what he had accomplished at the end of the day and could make some individual judgments on the job, such as how to stack storage materials. These features are unusual for un- skilled work.

The night shift, common in many unskilled jobs, is a feature with ill consequences. One study found that people "seem to be most irritable when they work nights."[8] Dissatis- faction with night work is also evidenced by high turnover and absentee rates.

For workers long employed in unskilled jobs, the marks of maladjustment are often unmistakable. They include feel- ings that can be described with such words as powerlessness, persecution, deprivation, insecurity, anxiety, depression, hope- lessness, and despair. A sociologist defines "feelings of power- lessness" as a firm conviction that one has no influence "over one's own affairs—a sense that the things that importantly affect one's activities and work are outside his control."[9] Discussing this statement, another writer comments: "The idea is that the worker is not being challenged by his work, that the incentive has been taken out of his job. Work for him is naked performance, while others make decisions."[10]

Unskilled jobs send back into the community people who have been psychologically assaulted and whose feelings and attitudes reflect such mistreatment. The psychological wounds produced by the job affect behavior away from work—in family life, social relations, and other respects.

The Special Case of Black Workers

The damaging consequences of working in unskilled jobs for long periods apply to both young and old, males and females, whites and blacks. For black workers, however, the consequences are likely to be most severe.

Both white and black workers desire jobs that carry some prestige, and are unhappy in positions that do not. A study concluded: "Contrary to popular belief, our data reveal a remarkable similarity between white workers and black workers in their desire for work that carries social prestige. An overwhelming majority of both black and white workers want work that is at least respected by the people they know."[11] There is some evidence that job prestige is more important to black workers than to white. A journal article pointed out that a decent job is particularly important to blacks because they have long been subjected to discrimination and now have a special need to "prove themselves." Accordingly, many blacks are anxious to overcome the inferiority image that society has placed upon them and to break out of their long–held position of second–class citizen.[12]

A book about two black policemen working together in a ghetto recounts many observations they made that illustrate the emphasis of blacks upon prestige. Sitting in their patrol car, they saw black men going to work in the morning. "A few men climb the El stairs; they all seemed to carry attaché cases. 'Janitors,' Smitty guesses. 'Yeah, they carry coveralls in the cases; that's how bad they need some dignity,' Hutch said in his emotional voice."[13]

Another reason why black workers find unskilled jobs particularly undesirable is because they realize their chances of advancement are very poor compared to the opportunities available to their white peers. They know that they are likely to be stuck in their menial job for a very long period, and this heightens their dissatisfaction. At a Senate hearing on employment in the cities, Senator Harris of Oklahoma commented on the plight of unskilled black workers. "They think about careers and jobs that lead to something, just as we members of the middle class do. I held menial jobs, as many of you did, when I was growing up, but I doubt if you could have got me interested in such jobs if I had known that I was going to be condemned to working at them for the rest of my life." Later on in the hearing, Congressman James Corbit of California reinforced what Senator Harris said: "I do not think there are any of us who did not go through a period of his life where he had a menial job to do for a little wage. But each of us knew that it was temporary. It was a step toward something much better. For a young Negro who looks at the adults around him and sees that they never moved out of those positions, it is quite a different thing."[14] The discontent that black workers feel in performing menial jobs has been documented by many studies, including that of the 108 workers conducted by this author that will be reported in the final section of this chapter.

Beyond expressing dissatisfaction with their menial jobs, many blacks react by losing interest in working or by accepting a job without any real degree of commitment. "Less than satisfactory work habits among new recruits and trainees," commented a personnel analyst, "may be more a function of adjustment problems and fear of dead–end jobs than disaffection from work norms."[15] The observer reached this conclusion following a survey that revealed "only a very small minority of black workers have renounced the widely accepted values of work held in this society."[16]

The young, unskilled black who accepts his first unskilled job often starts out with good intentions. But after he performs the same menial tasks day after day, week after week, after he sees that he is earning and learning little from what he is doing, and after he realizes that he has few chances of moving up to a better job, he often simply loses interest. A manpower report to the President of the United States stated: "The Negro youth starts out with determination to do a good job, but experience with a number of menial, low–paying and insecure jobs quickly produces an erosion of his commitment to work."[17]

This statement brings up another factor, the insecurity of unskilled jobs. Most unskilled black workers are acutely aware that they can be easily replaced since almost anyone can perform their jobs. They also realize that their jobs may be eliminated as plant operations become increasingly mechanized and automated. Unskilled jobs presently are being eliminated at a rapid rate which is expected to increase in the future. The National Commission on Technology, Automation, and Economic Progress has pointed out that, in order for the unemployment rate to be brought to a common level, blacks must gain access to the rapidly growing higher skilled and white–collar occupations at a faster rate in the future.

Another reason why unskilled black workers seem to be more discontented with menial jobs than white workers is because blacks have a stronger sense of group identity than whites. One proof of this is that when a black man becomes famous in a particular field, a sense of pride spreads quickly throughout the black community. According to Dick Gregory, when James Meredith became the first black man to enter an all white Southern college, the majority of blacks in America identified very closely with him. "Negroes looked a little different and acted a little different when all were graduated with him, graduated from the derogatory statement that all Negroes are ignorant, that all Negroes are lazy, that all Negroes stink."[18]

Within factories where unskilled blacks work, they are quick to form cliques. Since most black workers in a particular plant live in the same ghetto community, they often maintain close contact both on the job and after working hours. They are thus able to discuss their common problems at their work places as well as in their neighborhoods. This often leads to an acute awareness of mutual grievances and a corresponding intensification of group discontent.

One other factor that leads blacks to empathize with each other and internalize collective problems is that they share a common historical background. "Whether employed or unemployed, Negro workers," according to one social historian, "have little prestige; in addition, their lack of skills, education, and employment historically left them with little talent. Lack of influence plus the presence of racial isolation were partly responsible for their maintaining a sub–culture reminiscent of their Southern, agrarian origin."[19]

The black power movement of the 1960's brought an even greater sense of identity and awareness of mutual problems among blacks. The movement brought long–standing problems into sharp focus and made blacks aware of the unenviable situation they shared in society and the obstacles involved in altering it. "Young Negroes who are highly identified with the black power movement," stated Professor Eli Ginzberg in 1968, "simply do not believe that the civil rights revolution that they have been waiting for is fulfilled when they can get a job for $1.60 as a dishwasher, and when they suspect that ten years hence they may still be in that same job."[20]

Blacks in menial jobs often feel that their employment status is simply another reflection of their second–class citizenship. An unskilled black worker interviewed by the author said: "The factory reinforces the unequal system. They have you on the bottom and they keep you there."

Most black workers are convinced that even if better jobs should open up where they work, they will be judged on the basis of their color rather than on their capability. The difference between the attitudes of white and black workers regarding advancement opportunity has been documented in study after study. Black workers see one indication of prejudice and discrimination as being that, as one worker observed, "Whites want Negroes who talk, dress, and look like them." It has indeed been true for blacks that the lighter one's skin, the further one could hope to go. It is also a fact that a black worker with a "natural" hair style has practically sealed off his chances of advancement in many organizations.

As a result of the discrimination they see facing them, black unskilled workers are not only discontent with their work, but distrustful of those for whom they work. As one report on a training program involving 19 black men noted, "Negroes' expectations are, on the whole, reality–based. His problem in the training situation was that he had a backlog of expectations of maltreatment accompanied by an inability to sort out who was sincere and who was not, who was to be trusted and who was not."[21]

Attitudes and Perceptions of Black Workers:
Survey Results

The survey of 108 black workers that was conducted by this writer produced additional data regarding the attitudes and perceptions of black unskilled workers. Ninety percent of them, as of the black paraprofessionals interviewed, deemed their jobs important to the organizations where they work. This perception of the importance of the unskilled jobs holds true regardless of place of work. Black unskilled workers in hospitals did not see their work as any more important to the organization than their counterparts in private plants. Most of the hospital workers saw themselves as being important because they "have responsibility to see that the patients get the correct food," or because they performed other duties related to patient care. The plant workers, meanwhile, said their jobs were important because they played a necessary role in helping to produce quality products.

While black unskilled workers and paraprofessionals

agree in viewing their jobs as important, a distinction between the two groups is apparent. The unskilled worker believes that he himself is expendable; only 30 percent of the unskilled workers interviewed felt that it would be "difficult" to replace them, while 50 percent of the paraprofessionals felt this way. Only one of the 32 paraprofessionals interviewed thought it would "not be difficult at all" to replace him, as compared to four unskilled workers who gave this response.

This difference between the way unskilled workers and paraprofessionals view their self–worth as workers was also revealed in answers to the question of whether they thought they could be replaced by a machine. Fifty–nine percent of the unskilled workers thought that this was either "very possible" or "somewhat possible." Only 6 percent of the paraprofessionals felt this way.

As discussed previously, a large majority of unskilled workers are convinced they do not possess any special ability needed to perform their jobs. Why then do they view the job itself as important? One possible explanation is that when a worker contemplates the functional importance of his job, he does not think in terms of the entire company, but only of the operations surrounding his immediate position. The assembly line packer, for example, considers his job necessary to keeping the conveyor belt running smoothly, though he probably sees his work as having little significance to the entire company. The unskilled worker may therefore rate his job as being important while at the same time considering himself easily replaceable. As one worker commented, "The clean up work must be done. Someone has to do it." The majority of workers who classified their jobs as important indeed complained that "it carries no status."

The above findings may be indicative of a detachment or alienation that unskilled workers feel toward their jobs. They are apparently performing their job without internalizing what they are doing and not really feeling a part of it. This explains how a worker can regard his job as important while seeing himself as not necessary to it. He performs the job mechanically and does not see himself adding anything special to it that no one else could give to it, not even a "machine."

If the unskilled worker is truly detached from his work, this helps to explain why he does not seem to gain the same satisfaction from it as the paraprofessionals interviewed. While 37 percent of the unskilled workers said they often thought about other kinds of work they would rather be doing, only 9 percent of the higher–level workers admitted to this. Furthermore, 22 percent of the lower–level workers specified that they thought about other jobs "very often." While 75 percent of the workers in higher–level jobs reported having "rarely" or "never" thought about another kind of work, only one out of three of the workers in unskilled jobs answered this way.

In commenting on why they disliked their jobs, one of the unskilled workers said, "It is not challenging, it is routine." Yet the paraprofessionals often spoke about their work as being "challenging, interesting, and meaningful" or said that they liked their job because they enjoyed coming "to work dressed up, meeting important people, and telling other people what to do."

In addition to not gaining satisfaction from the job because of monotonous duties, the unskilled worker does not perceive his job as something personal to himself. He tries not to take his job into consideration in forming his self–identity. When a lawyer thinks about himself he usually considers his occupation as a major component of himself. But a dishwasher may wash dishes one week, do stock work the next, and clean floors after that. He can only consider himself an unskilled, low–paid worker. It is therefore to be expected that he will constantly think about other jobs he would rather be doing.

Other questions in the survey revealed that unskilled workers find it difficult to develop a liking for and attachment to their jobs. While 57 percent of the unskilled workers surveyed felt they would miss their work either only "a little bit" or "not at all" if transferred to another job, all of the paraprofessionals said they would miss their jobs at least "some-what" if transferred, and most said "a great deal." In other words, none of the higher–level workers was ambivalent about his work, while over half of the unskilled workers were.

Further dissatisfaction among unskilled workers was noted in their tendency to see the company as underpaying and exploiting them. In discussing their wages, 59 percent felt they were too low for what they were doing. A lesser per-centage (50%) of the paraprofessional workers thought they were being underpaid. While the unskilled workers often wanted another job with "more money," several parapro-fessionals desired to keep their jobs precisely because of "pay security."

It appears that the unskilled workers in the plant setting were more content with their work than the unskilled hospital workers. It was found that 72 percent of the plant workers would miss their organization "somewhat" to a "great deal" if transferred, while only about 57 percent of the hospital workers held this view. Plant workers were also apparently able to become more involved in their work. When asked if their work helped them to forget worries and problems, 56 percent of the plant workers answered "a great deal" compared to 39 percent of the hospital workers who gave this response. In fact, of the hospital workers, 18 percent felt their work did not help at all, compared to only 9 percent of the plant workers who felt this way.

The aspiration level of the unskilled workers was found to be high, as was that of the paraprofessionals. Both groups, however, appeared to lack the confidence to take the action necessary to fulfill these aspirations. While 71 percent of the unskilled workers felt that there was another job in the com-pany that they would have liked to have and thought they could do, only 16 percent had ever tried to get it. A smaller percentage (37%) identified jobs outside the organization which they would like to have and for which they thought they were qualified. Still, less than half of the workers who felt this way had tried to get the job. This reluctance is prob-

ably due partly to a lack of self–confidence in unskilled workers. But because paraprofessionals felt similarly, and since
both groups are black, part of the explanation may be that
these workers expected to encounter racial discrimination
that would block their advancement.

When the responses of workers are compared by place of
work, a large majority from both hospitals and plants seemed
to feel there was a better job both within and outside their
company which they would have liked to have and believed
they were qualified to perform. While small percentages of
both groups had ever tried to get the desired job outside the
company, a greater proportion of hospital workers (21%)
than plant workers (9%) had tried to get the desired job
within their organization. This may mean that black workers
in an institutional setting may see a better chance for advancement than their counterparts in private industry. This is understandable in view of the fact that blacks have traditionally
found it easier to obtain positions of importance in public
agencies and institutions. Statistics indeed reveal more blacks
in high-level positions in public and institutional places than
in other work settings.

A high percentage of both unskilled and paraprofessional
workers were found to be interested in taking part in a training program. Yet a larger percentage of the paraprofessionals
(16%) were not interested in participating in such a program
than the unskilled workers (4%). Interviews with workers
revealed that this may be due to the fact that many higher–
level workers feel that their training takes place as they perform their jobs and that they do not see a need for a formal
training program to enable them to develop their skills.

7

FAMILY LIFE AND COMMUNITY INVOLVEMENT

The consequences for black workers of confinement to menial jobs go beyond the work setting. In their adjustment to family life, their relations with friends and neighbors, and their participation in social groups, the impact of the job is apparent.

Some Overall Observations

Many of the psychological consequences of menial work discussed in the previous chapter have been studied by social scientists concerned with the after–work lives of the working poor. The studies have amply documented that their family life and social relations are in many ways a reflection of on–the–job frustrations. Some of their social involvements take on a deprived and impoverished character. Others exist as a form of compensation for the adverse psychological effects of their jobs.

Focusing on the first type of social involvements, studies have found that the most deprived workers are less stable in their social contacts than other workers and that emotional insecurity produced by confinement to menial jobs is transformed off the job into social instability.[1]

Sociologist Ely Chinoy in his classic study of workers in an automobile factory found that assembly–line workers at the end of the workday were physically and psychologically exhausted and incapable of lively and creative after–work activities.[2] Harold Wilensky observed the same pattern, labeling it "the spillover leisure syndrome." He adopted the term after observing that unskilled workers "developed a spillover leisure routine in which alienation from work becomes alienation from life; the mental stultification produced by their labor permeated their leisure."[3]

Other studies have found that after–work social activities sometimes take the form of attempted compensation for the gratification the unskilled worker is deprived of at work. The greater the psychological deprivation caused by the job, the greater is the desire for a rewarding home–life.[4]

Such desire to gain satisfaction after work often takes on an almost desperate character. One study found that people in menial jobs actively participate in clubs and other social organizations. It concluded that "the opportunity to engage in something creative, even if only a hobby association, provides a compensation for the deadening effect of working on a simple repetitive task."[5] Another study found that after work social contacts are extremely important to unskilled workers because of the absence of meaningful social relations on the job.[6] Evidence is presented in another work that "the community that springs up on the shop floor is not of great moment to the production worker, although his membership in it and liking for it may be essential in permitting him to get through the day."[7] Social relations at work, the author observes, are neither deep, permanent, nor very gratifying for menial job holders. They are not very meaningful because, on the one hand, the work situation permits only fragmentary and shallow social interaction, while on the other, the workers themselves do not want more than superficial and temporary relations because of their negative feelings about their overall work environment.

Ironically, many unskilled workers do not very actively

seek the gratifying experiences off the job that they so deeply desire. Many such workers have been observed to be timid, reserved, and reluctant to try new experiences. From their slight gratification on the job, they appear to fear that they will be similarly disappointed in other situations. And many who do actively pursue after-work activities, engage in activities that are likely to be neither well planned nor very purposive. One study used the word "aimlessness" to describe this pattern of indirection.[8]

Perhaps, as has been suggested in one study, the aimlessness found in the after–work lives of many unskilled workers is due to the feelings of powerlessness and hopelessness produced by the job. These feelings, the study claims, are transformed off the job into a failure to plan for the future and a concern with living for today and for obtaining gratification from such material goods as television sets and cars and from immediate excitement, as opposed to longer–term or more abstract goals.[9]

The low wages paid to unskilled workers adversely affect their family life and even family stability. Bayard Rustin, in discussing the high frequency of abandonment by husbands in low–income families, points out that many men "purposely move out on their families because they cannot support them on $35, $40, $50 a week. And it is because they leave home, because they desert their families, that the $400 or $500 a month necessary for the family to survive can come in from relief."[10]

Besides affecting family life, low wages can limit social involvements and leisure activities for which money is needed. In this category are many primary–group activities with relatives and friends that demand material or social reciprocity and membership in social or religious organizations which require dues or donations.

The insecurity of menial work and the tendency of workers to move from one job to another have definite after–work consequences. Job instability, according to the classic sociologist Emile Durkheim, conditions a person to rapid shifts in social values and changing group relations and thus discourages loyalties and attachments to all social groups. As a result, the person often regards all groups as unstable and subject to rapid change.[11]

Because standing in the community is determined largely by occupation, unskilled workers are assigned to a very low social stratum. An occupation is generally awarded prestige according to the income it brings and the specialized training it requires. Thus, unskilled jobs confer little prestige on their holders. The social relations of menial jobholders are confined to others in the lower social strata.

Frank Riessman has drawn a portrait of the "underprivileged" person that summarizes much of what has been said about the social and psychological consequences of menial work. Riessman characterizes the "underprivileged" person as one who is alienated from society, has a strong desire for excitement in order to "get away from the humdrum of daily life," is pragmatic and anti–intellectual, is more inclined to act physically rather than think things out (an indication, says Riessman, of his principal economic assets of strength and endurance), and who places a great emphasis on masculinity, regarding talk, reading, and intellectual activities as unmasculine.[12]

Findings of the Survey

Many of the findings of other studies were confirmed in the survey of 108 black workers conducted by this writer. Some new insights also resulted. That working in a menial job can significantly affect a worker's family life is shown by the finding that 31.6 percent of the unskilled workers interviewed said they often come home from work too tired to enjoy doing things with their family. This was reported only rarely by the comparison group of higher–level paraprofessional workers who were surveyed.

Although the unskilled workers may come home from work exhausted, it was nevertheless found that they tend to discuss their jobs with their family at least as frequently as the higher–level workers who were interviewed. The data showed that 54 percent of the unskilled workers talked to their families "often" about their jobs compared with 50 percent of the para-professionals. But a large difference was found between the two groups of workers in after–work social involvements. While only 43 percent of the unskilled workers belonged to a community organization, 81 percent of the higher–level work-ers were members. Furthermore, the paraprofessionals greatly outnumbered the unskilled workers in the *number* of organiza-tions to which they belonged. In all, 56 percent of the higher–level workers belonged to three or more organizations, while this was true of only 7 percent of the unskilled workers.

The nonmembers in both the unskilled and the parapro-fessional groups were compared in terms of their desire to join a social organization. All of the paraprofessionals but only about half of the unskilled workers who were not members of a social organization expressed a desire to join one.

Although some relationship was expected between mem-bership in unions and involvement in social organizations, none was found to exist. The data revealed that an equal number of union and nonunion members alike (about 30%) wish to join a social organization.

While union membership does not seem to have a bearing on organization participation, certain job factors appear to be related. For example, workers who have been frustrated in trying to obtain a better job have veered away from participa-tion in organizations. It appears that, having experienced fail-ure in the work setting, they are inclined to limit their involve-ments after hours. Workers who were frustrated in trying to get a better job and workers who did not make an attempt were compared in the number of organization memberships. It was found that only 36% of the frustrated workers belonged to at least one organization, while 60 percent of the others were organization members. Similarly, only 14 percent of the frustrated workers who are not organization members desire membership, while 36 percent of the others do.

8

POLITICAL PARTICIPATION

Aristotle observed that man is a political animal. In stating this, he recognized that some type of participation in both formal and informal political endeavors is a central human activity. This is especially true in a democracy such as America with an ideology that encourages broad–based political participation.

This chapter focuses upon the political behavior of the working poor. The concern is with the nature and extent of their participation in political processes and their attitudes toward political issues and institutions.

The Political Structure and the Working Poor

There is much evidence that menial, low–paying jobs play a part in shaping the political behavior of people who occupy them. One researcher who found that the unskilled workers he studied showed a high degree of political apathy and alienation, explained this in terms of the "psychic and· social withdrawal" produced by the job.[1]

After reviewing the many studies of political behavior

that take into account employment factors the conclusion can
be drawn that unskilled workers seem to be alienated from traditional political institutions and are generally passive in their
performance of the citizen role. Voting studies have found that
blacks, the group that predominates in unskilled jobs, exercise
their right to vote less frequently than whites.

Holders of unskilled jobs spend a large part of their wak-
ing hours in large, impersonal work settings. Given their low
position, they have little influence there and rules are simply
handed down for them to obey. The regimentation, imperson-
ality, and nondemocratic process go a long way to condition
them to be politically passive. A study of workers in the Detroit
area found that the unskilled firmly believed that they had a
minimal amount of power when confronted with the political
structure. "In some degree feelings of political futility," the
book concluded, "are merely an extension or special application of the general pessimistic and despairing outlook."[2]

Besides the effect of the work setting, the job itself can
add to political alienation. One study found that stagnation on
the job promotes a willingness to accept the *status quo* off the
job. Such acceptance, it was found, negates all desire to bring
about change.[3] Other research supports the point that "a man
who may be a disinterested worker may also be content to be
regulated by the routine requirements of his employment, and
he may be uneasy during days away from work when the
discipline of the routine is absent. . . . An imposed time–use
routine relieves the individual of making decisions about what
he should do, where he should be and when."[4]

It has also been found that the high degree of insecurity
combined with the low self–esteem of unskilled workers makes
them wary of dealing with power systems and power figures.
Michael Harrington has commented that the working poor
are passive, inert, and apathetic, lacking the desire and capacity for political organization and action.[5] But sociologist S. M.
Miller does not agree, pointing out that residents of low–
income neighborhoods have engaged in many political actions
and have had numerous successes in their political endeavors.

He argues that all of the major problems of such neighborhoods are really political issues and points out that concerted attempts by residents to do something about them have not been uncommon.[6]

But the attempts of such residents to solve community problems often do not follow conventional methods. Viewing government as something largely beyond their control, they are alienated from the existing political structure and skeptical of the standard political channels. The result is often a desire for radical reforms and a sympathy for rebellious actions. There are many historical instances in which "militant workmen have supported a revolutionary party," an authority notes.[7] Besides doubting that conventional political processes are responsive to them, the working poor seriously question the qualifications and effectiveness of public officials and question whether political institutions are equipped to solve major national and international problems.

Thus it is argued that while unskilled workers are largely apathetic to the conventional political system, their substantial discontent causes them to sympathize with radical movements. Accordingly, one political writer concludes that the consequences of confinement to menial work "are not very healthy for a democratic policy."[8] Another, focusing on unskilled mass–production workers, finds that the present low standing of this occupational category is a recent phenomenon. The mass–production worker, he points out, enjoyed a relatively high status in the period between World War I and the Korean War. Since many blacks held such jobs then, as they do now, he argues that the previous higher status represented an upsurge in the socioeconomic status and political power of the black American. "In fact," he comments, "the civil rights victories, beginning with the Supreme Court decision in 1954 which outlaws segregated schools, were largely a consequence of the tremendous gains the Negro had made socially, economically, and politically as a mass–production worker. . . ." With the end of the Korean War, he claims that a major setback to the black American occurred.[9]

Factors Affecting Political Behavior: Survey Findings

The survey of black workers conducted by the author provides evidence of low political participation among unskilled workers. Only 76 percent of the unskilled workers were registered to vote, as against 91 percent of the paraprofessionals. Over two thirds of the unskilled workers not registered qualified to register. All of the registered paraprofessionals said they had voted in the last election; in contrast, only 84 percent of the registered unskilled workers reported voting. When the nonvoters were asked about their failure, the responses clearly reflected apathy. Two "just forgot to vote," two found it "too inconvenient," three were "not interested," and two were undecided on the candidates. All told, 36 percent of the unskilled workers had not voted in the last election, compared to only 9 percent of the paraprofessionals.

Several factors that conceivably could have an effect on voting tendency were examined. Since workers in hospitals and plants participated in elections in about equal percentages, it appears that place of work does not influence voting behavior. On the other hand, the survey indicated a relationship between workers' participation in and attitudes toward unions and their participation in voting. While 83 percent of the union members voted in the last election, only 56 percent of the nonunion members voted. Members may be more sensitive to election issues through information received from their unions. Moreover, they may have more reason to vote because of group pressure and a strong sense of group identification. A member votes to benefit his union on many issues from which the isolated individual feels apart. The effect of seemingly remote issues on a large organization to which one belongs is easier to see than their effect on oneself individually. Finally, a union member is likely to feel that as part of a large bloc he has more influence in voting. A study of workers in the Detroit area indeed found that they identified with their unions on election issues, and in fact, that they trusted unions for advice more than the church, veterans, and fraternal groups to which they belonged.[10]

Other data in the present survey revealed that members involved in union affairs are more likely to be politically active than those less involved. Thus, voting in the last general election were 93 percent of the members who did and only 70 percent of the members who did not vote in union elections.

In addition to union membership and union voting as factors influencing political participation, workers who feel they are receiving good union representation are less apathetic politically than workers who feel the reverse. Significantly, the survey disclosed that all of the workers who responded with "strongly agree" to the suggestion that they were receiving good union representation voted in the last election, 83 percent who merely responded "agree" voted, and 50 percent of the workers who felt they were *not* getting good union representation voted. Workers who find fault with their union representation have possibly become alienated from the mainstream of union activities and feel they belong to a powerless minority. Perhaps they feel that the representation they may expect in government as a result of voting will also be less than satisfactory.

Experiences on the job also appear to be important in influencing political participation. The survey showed that 36 percent of workers frustrated in seeking a better job did not vote in the last election, as against 21 percent of the nonfrustrated. Another finding of relevance is that workers who were more aggressive when faced with problems with their supervisors were less politically apathetic; 85 percent of this group had voted in the last election and only 25 percent of the workers who retreated from such problems had voted.

Job satisfaction is another factor that seems to affect political participation. Of those workers who said they felt like a "somebody" at work 78 percent voted in the last election; only 50 percent of the workers who saw themselves as a "nobody" voted.

In trying to determine awareness of public issues, workers were asked how often they read a newspaper. It was found

that the higher–level paraprofessionals kept themselves significantly more informed than the unskilled workers. Ninety–one
percent of the paraprofessionals read a newspaper daily, compared to only 70 percent of the unskilled workers. It was
found, however, that unskilled workers (26%) are twice as
much inclined to read black newspapers as the paraprofessionals (13%) (both groups in the survey, it should be remembered, are black). This finding could indicate that the
alienation of unskilled workers from the total political spec-
trum gives them a more restricted view of their environment
and focuses their attention more on their own ethnic group
and immediate surroundings.

9

TRAPPED IN THE GHETTO

"Cities are the sink of the human race," said 18th Century philosopher Jean-Jacques Rousseau. In the 20th Century, United States President Lyndon B. Johnson said: "We know that cities can stimulate the best in man, and aggravate the worst."[1] What is negative in these statements does not apply so much to entire cities as to the slum pockets within them. Today, in the United States, such slum pockets exist mainly as black ghettos.

Although all people who live in a ghetto endure many hardships, evidence has been assembled in this chapter to show that ghetto inhabitants in unskilled, dead–end jobs react particularly negatively to their living environment. First a description of the contemporary black ghetto is in order.

Conditions in the Black Ghetto

Albert Black, chairman of the Newark Commission for Human Rights, has spoken of the black ghetto of Newark as "the rotten casket destined for the burial of the living dead."[2] A more detailed description of the black ghetto is provided by a black urbanologist who states: "The black ghetto is more than a place; it is a condition. The black ghetto is not just a

slum, although a slum may be and frequently is the location of
the ghetto." A slum, he further explains, is a deteriorated part
of the city where housing, recreation facilities, and government services are substandard. But more than this, "the black
ghetto is a section of the city which has enforced boundaries,
visible or invisible, which shut in people of one race and mini-
mize their contacts with the larger society as effectively as did
the island community of the original ghetto. . . ."[3]

Some observers of the contemporary black ghetto say that
its very existence is a reflection of the racist character of our
society. "The deeper tragedy," this authority comments, "is
that the same sentiments that conceive the black ghetto as a
proper residential reservation for blacks, conceive and enforce
other reservations in employment, education, religious life, and
the administration of justice. Racism is like hydrophobia: You
can't have just a little of it."[4] This point of view holds that the
substantial racism that exists in the United States is at once
reflected in the black ghetto as well as responsible for its perpetuation. "Educational segregation," comments a city planner, "results from residential segregation, insuring that Negroes will attend inferior schools. Inferior training means employment handicaps. Poor employment opportunities mean
lower income, and lower income means less buying power for
poor homes, and so the cycle is unbreakable."[5]

Because of inadequate services and deteriorating conditions in the black ghetto, a multitude of problems are faced
by the residents. The most basic is mere physical survival.
The ghetto resident has been confronted with an uphill struggle in efforts to maintain his health and personal safety.
Compared with residents of other areas, he frequently has
a shorter life expectancy, a greater likelihood of contract-
ing contagious illnesses, and generally poorer health. Health
care for blacks has been found to be consistently inferior to
that available to whites. Evidence is cited in a Federal report
which stated that blacks made far fewer visits for medical and
dental care than whites. This pattern held constant regardless
of income level, indicating that black ghettos contain poorer

and fewer health facilities than other areas. Blacks were also found to be receiving their medical care mostly in hospital clinics, as compared to whites who commonly obtained the care of private physicians.[6] Infant mortality rate, often considered the best single indicator of community health, is significantly higher in black ghettos than elsewhere.

Not only in the matter of health, but also in housing, education, employment, and recreation, living in the ghetto involves many hardships. Typical housing structures are substandard and deteriorated. And even these poor excuses for homes are usually not the property of their residents but of outsiders. The absentee ownership has had two unfortunate consequences. First, the dwellers feel little responsibility for the upkeep of the property and are in fact often resentful toward the owners. One study found that "renters tend to be less responsible than home–owners for the protection and improvement of property values and for community upkeep and betterment of practically every kind."[7] A second consequence is that landlords frequently exploit their tenants. Noting the prevalence of this in Newark's black ghettos, a local writer commented: "Anyone who knew the city was aware that owners of slum property gouged these tenants mercilessly."[8]

The post–World War II urban renewal program was launched as a Federal effort to improve the housing stock in the ghetto. But many observers now agree that many city urban renewal plans have been ill–conceived and have taken an excessively long time to implement if carried out at all. An example often cited is the Hough area of Cleveland, which was leveled for urban renewal and then remained undeveloped for more than ten years. "So many buildings had been toppled and cleared away by the middle 1960s," commented one observer, "that visitors to the city, lacking background information, invariably were startled by the scene of the destruction. Some of them with a more humanitarian streak, had to be restrained from summoning the Red Cross to the scene of obvious disaster."[9]

When urban renewal does succeed in providing a quantity of new housing in the ghetto, the results are often disappointing. Nathan Wright tells the story of a little girl riding in a car on the New Jersey Turnpike who took notice of Newark's skyline. She asked her mother: "What are those buildings that look like boxes?" "A city project," the mother answered; and the girl said: "Oh, I know what you mean, mother, a city jail." "Had the inquirer been several miles closer," suggests Wright, "she would have understood more clearly the uncanny wisdom of her seemingly innocent remark. The public housing projects of the nation, by and large, are like semisanitary dungeons that make men feel that they are less than men."[10]

Public housing projects are indeed often designed with little regard to aesthetic appearance or human values. They also frequently lack many simple features that would make them eminently more livable. Dick Gregory claims that one small artifact missing in most public housing projects, a doorbell in the lobby, contributes to the economic hardship of the tenants.

> Imagine you are a bill collector sent to make a collection in one of the new housing projects. Since there are no doorbells on the ground floor of the housing project, you must go up 20 stories to the individual apartment to find out if anyone is home. Most of the time the elevators are out of order, so you may have to walk. After you have walked up 20 flights of stairs you discover no one is home. If the same pattern continues with your next six customers, you return to your office without having made a single collection. You are tired and weary and do not want to go through the same process the next day, so you put a garnishee on your customer's salary.[11]

The type and quality of housing in the ghetto represents one major problem; the situation that exists in the area of employment constitutes another. A 1972 manpower report of the President found that the unemployment rate in the ghetto was nearly double the national average. Consistent with this, the report disclosed an almost two–to–one ratio in joblessness between blacks and whites. On top of this, a distressing trend was reported: "The unemployment rate for Negro workers continued to edge upward in 1971, while the rate for white workers leveled off. . . ."[12]

A study of poverty areas found that ghetto residents experience frequent periods of unemployment between their menial and unrewarding jobs and suffer a higher unemployment rate than the worst national rates since the depression period.[13] The Urban Coalition of New York City used this fact for a slogan aimed at increasing public awareness—"It's still 1930 in the ghetto."

As if matters in the ghetto were not bad enough, outsiders come to exploit its residents. Many small businesses that ghetto residents rely upon for essential goods and services are operated by outsiders. Many offer inferior merchandise at high prices and use the vehicle of "easy credit" to take further advantage of customers. Such practices as having customers sign incomplete loan agreements or selling them used merchandise as new add to the exploitation. Residents remain steady customers of these stores because they do not have the means to travel outside to do their shopping. Many are either unaware that they are being exploited or do not believe other white businessmen outside their area will treat them more fairly.[14] In a survey of businessmen in the poverty area of Mount Vernon, New York, conducted for the Mount Vernon Model Cities Agency, it was found that almost half (47%) of the retail merchants viewed competition for sales as either moderate or nonexistent. Moreover, over 90 percent of the merchants indicated that most of their business was from repeat customers.[15]

Many businessmen in the ghetto not only exploit black residents, but discriminate against them as well. This is apparent in that many white–owned ghetto businesses do not hire black employees. Black community leaders have reacted to this by advocating: "Don't buy where you can't work."[16]

In addition to being frustrated in their attempts to work for local business establishments, many residents who would like to establish a small business in the community are often prevented by the lack of substantial capital and business experience.

Not only are present ghetto conditions distressing, but prospects for the future are not very bright. Despite several government assistance programs, the 1960's brought little relief to the ghetto, while many conditions actually worsened. In several ghetto areas the incidence of poverty increased, the proportion of broken homes went up, and the high male unemployment rate remained constant.[17] Many questions are now being raised as to the effectiveness of government programs in the ghetto. There is particular pessimism among ghetto residents who have seen the failure of program after program in the past. The rapid ghetto population growth due to both steady in–migration and a high birth rate[18] also gives cause for concern.

The ghetto climate often stifles motivation to participate in and attempt to control mechanisms that can lead to community change. One commentary on ghetto residents speaks to this point: "They learn the uselessness of 'drive' and of education, the impossibility of finding either jobs or help on the other side of the wall."[19]

Government programs aimed at increasing the involvement of ghetto residents in improvement efforts have come up against this apathy, and for the most part have not been able to overcome it. A project in Washington, D.C. had as one of its objectives the goal of "getting people to feel that they can have a voice in their future." This effort proved to be a major undertaking, for it soon became clear that apathy was more widespread than at first apparent. In 1964, when a constitutional amendment gave the District of Columbia its first chance to vote for a U.S. President, only 25 percent of the eligible ghetto residents voted.[20]

Though massive problems in the ghetto contribute substantially to apathy, there are features which, although not formally recognized as problems, contribute as well. One study found that ghetto residents are faced with extreme loneliness. This was found to be particularly true in the case of children and often continues into adulthood. This loneliness, according to the study, results in a feeling of isolation and a lack of attachment to others.[21]

The pattern of black pockets of poverty surrounded by white neighborhoods of relative affluence is the same in virtually every city. Nathan Wright described it in Newark:

> In the face of the precipitous black migration to Newark, the white population has moved in two directions. It has moved into the suburbs and it has entrenched itself in several sections of the city... Seven of Newark's 12 neighborhoods have reflected a pattern of white entrenchment or a holding of the line against an "invasion" by the growing black population. These communities form almost a complete ring around the central core of Newark where the overwhelming majority of the city's black population resides.[22]

Besides problems of employment, education, and limited community resources caused by segregation, segregation in and by itself can have the effect of producing apathy. A recent study found that blacks living in an all black community tend to detach themselves from the mainstream of society more than blacks who live in integrated communities. The segregated blacks more often expressed feelings of alienation and passivity.[23]

Another characteristic of the ghetto is the small amount of political influence it wields. In his study of Newark, Nathan Wright examined a series of city issues on which the black ghetto held a definite position. He traced the outcome to determine the extent to which the preferences of the black community prevailed; in none did it achieve its goal.[24]

Political historians agree that the poor have traditionally been the least politically influential group. And most ghetto residents are poor. Their lack of wealth gives them little power, and politicians do not listen to the powerless. One observer notes: "The chronic poor have no connections; they are neither members of nor have any influence on the policy–making boards of the school, welfare, police, urban renewal, or church organizations. . . . They are politically disconnected and emasculated."[25]

The black ghetto, some feel, has been politically impotent

for yet another reason. A substantial degree of instability is said to exist in the black ghetto, due in part to urban renewal projects which periodically disrupt neighborhoods. This often prevents powerful political coalitions from forming among residents, according to some observers. It is also claimed that white politicians often sponsor programs deliberately to fragment the black ghetto population. Tom Hayden charged: "The City's [Newark's] vast programs for urban renewal, highways, downtown development, and most recently a 150–acre medical school, in the heart of the ghetto, seemed almost deliberately designed to squeeze out this rapidly growing Negro community that represents a majority of the population."[26]

It was noted in a previous chapter that local governments have been losing many of their functions to the Federal government. Because ghettos are within the immediate jurisdiction of local governments, this trend has further contributed to the low degree of political influence of the ghetto. Senator Abraham A. Ribicoff of Connecticut has observed, "We have become so bureaucratic in our thinking, so concerned with metropolitan, regional and national scale, that we have forgotten about the neighborhood and the people living there." Even when ghetto residents are successful in joining together to form political coalitions, their influence rarely extends beyond local city government while many important decisions affecting their community are made in Washington.

An episode in Philadelphia serves as an example of local citizens succeeding in gaining influence in city government only to find that they were being ignored in higher and apparently more important quarters. A "Citizens' Council on City Planning" formed by local residents was influential with local government officials, but soon found that many of the decisions affecting their community lay in the hands of state and Federal officials who were beyond their reach.[27]

Many efforts to organize the ghetto community and to stimulate resident participation are staffed by outside middle–class individuals. Ghetto residents often feel they are being dominated or used by these people. The majority of public and private efforts to provide services to the ghetto are also usually staffed by nonresident personnel, of whom residents are often suspicious. It certainly seems that many social workers who represent a large contingent of the "helpers" in the ghetto are often more concerned with checking the qualifications of residents who request help rather than with actually helping them. In addition, the "helpers" often differ among themselves in goals and orientation. These divisions frequently lead to duplicated and uncoordinated efforts that ghetto residents may perceive as a lack of desire to help. Besides the divisions among the "helpers," disagreements may arise between the outsiders and the local community leaders, who often have a better sense of community feeling but frequently are not approached by the the outsiders for their views on approaches and methods.

The potential and need of the ghetto for economic development has been much discussed, along with the extent to which industry can help and will try to help. There are many gray areas concerning the desire of industry to assist impoverished areas, such as whether a "corporate social conscience" really exists. Few businessmen disagree that the main objective of business is to make a profit. Many even say that this is the only function of business.

Some businessmen have felt that the ghetto offers opportunities for industrial development and profit. Advantages of an industrial location there are the availability of labor and the central city site. It has been felt, however, that because of such difficulties as acquiring land and training unskilled people, special tax advantages and other government help should be offered as incentives to industry. Government has responded at both the national and local level by establishing a few incentive programs. Evidence exists to show that, beyond higher start–up costs, companies in the ghetto always operate at higher costs than those located elsewhere. One study found that despite the ample availability of labor in the ghetto, its cost to industry is as much as three times as high as elsewhere; factors responsible are a high worker turnover and the greater effort in training new employees.[28]

A report prepared by the Federal government found a large number of business failures in the ghetto and burdensomely high operating costs for newly established businesses that have survived. The report concluded that "the business environment of ghetto areas does not seem to be conducive to profit."[29] The Aero–Jet General plant in the Watts section of Los Angeles was one of the examples cited. The company was established in 1966 to manufacture tents. "In the first year," reported the study, "1,200 [people] had to be hired to maintain a work force of 500; and the company estimates that its training costs were closer to $5,000 per man than the $1,300 paid by the Labor Department to offset the costs of hiring and retraining ghetto residents."[30]

Reaction to Ghetto Conditions: Survey Findings

The survey conducted of 108 black workers yielded information on their perception of the ghetto conditions in which they lived. All saw problems in their community. Few respondents were at a loss for something to say when asked to name three major community problems. Below is a list of the most frequently cited:

1. Robbery	15. Depreciation of	27. Lack of trees
2. Vandalism	property values	28. Poor educational
3. Violence	16. Traffic hazards	facilities
4. Drinking	17. Noise level	29. Unqualified
5. Prostitution	18. Poor housing	teachers
6. Drug addiction	19. Dirt	30. Poor condition
7. Race relations	20. Rats	of sidewalks
8. Loitering	21. Urban clearance	31. Police problems
9. Unemployment	22. Poor street	32. Poor health
10. Poor jobs	lighting	services
11. Taxes	23. Stray dogs	33. Government
12. Apathy	24. Inadequate parks	unresponsiveness
13. Problem	25. Poor shopping	
teenagers	facilities	
14. Ineffective	26. Poor physical	
leadership	appearance	

The analysis of the survey data indicates that unskilled

workers are more concerned with problems which immediately affect them than with less tangible, longer–term environmental features. The higher–level black workers interviewed tended to be concerned with deeper and more abstract community problems. In general, however, they were more critical of their community than the lower–level jobholders. Both groups of workers lived in ghettos. The income difference between them was not great enough to permit the higher–level employees, the paraprofessionals, to escape. Living in the ghetto, side–by–side with the unskilled and/or the unemployed, the higher–level workers are likely to feel deprived, worthy of better surroundings, and understandably more critical of their environment.

The survey showed the higher–level workers also to be concerned mostly with nonphysical problems in their community, while the unskilled workers are critical primarily of immediate and physical aspects. Thus, the overwhelming majority of the paraprofessionals (72%) saw the community schools as fair to very poor, while 51 percent of the unskilled workers perceived them as good to excellent. The higher–level workers were also more critical of the police; only 19 percent rated them as good to excellent, as against 33 percent of the unskilled workers. The greater concern of the unskilled workers with immediate, more physical problems is shown by the finding that 36 percent of them rated public transportation as poor to very poor, compared to only 16 percent of the paraprofessionals. A full 34 percent of the unskilled workers and only 19 percent of the higher–level workers rated sanitation services as poor to very poor.

But as noted, the paraprofessionals tended to be generally more critical of their community. Over one third (38%) rated the housing as poor to very poor, in contrast to 25 percent of the unskilled. Also, 46 percent of the unskilled workers considered present health services in the community as good to excellent, with which only 28 percent of the paraprofessionals concurred. It is interesting that unskilled workers employed in hospitals saw community health service as being better than did workers holding jobs in plants; perhaps their jobs gave them some insights into the difficulties of providing proper health care. Or perhaps the hospital workers derive some self–esteem from feeling that these services are of high quality. It is similar to the General Electric Company employee who feels that GE products are best. Of the hospital workers, 55% rated the health services as good to excellent, while only 38% of the plant workers gave them this high rating.

The attitudes of workers were further determined by asking them to indicate the racial make–up of the neighborhood in which they would most prefer to live. The answers were used to determine their level of dissatisfaction with their present segregated, all black community. A large majority of workers from both occupational levels said they would prefer a racially mixed neighborhood. Only 5 percent of the unskilled workers and only 9 percent of the paraprofessionals indicated their preference was an all black neighborhood. One worker gave the following reason for this: "They don't want you around them." When those who preferred a mixed community were asked their reasons, the majority gave answers that indicated their feelings about the advantages of blacks and whites living together. One respondent said, "Because the world is mixed and I don't see isolating myself." Another commented, "So we can learn to get along with one another." Others wanted to move to a mixed area because they believed that the quality of white and mixed neighborhoods was higher than all black areas. As one worker said, "They have better housing and facilities."

The expectation that black workers who had good relations with whites on the job would tend to prefer living in a racially mixed neighborhood was confirmed. Twenty–six percent of the workers who did not believe racial discrimination existed at the job did not care about racial composition in selecting a community in which to live, while only 9 percent of the workers who perceived discrimination said they would not be concerned about this factor.

Another portion of the survey revealed that black workers with white supervisors have a greater desire to live in a mixed neighborhood than black workers with black supervisors. Eighty–one percent of the workers with white supervisors favored living in a mixed neighborhood, compared to only 63 percent of the workers with black supervisors. As one black worker with a white supervisor said: "I work with all types of people, so we should live together."

When workers were asked how they would feel if they suddenly had to move away from their present neighborhood, there was little difference in the answers of the unskilled and the paraprofessionals, with the majority of both groups saying they would feel "bad." There may have been a misinterpretation of this question which could be responsible for these results. Since it was not otherwise specified, many of the workers probably believed that the choice presented was that of moving out of one ghetto and into another, since this is the type of move to which most blacks are accustomed.

The attachment of workers to their community seems to be affected by their job. A relationship was found between attachment to one's job and one's community (as measured by reluctance to move to another community). Fifty–nine percent of the workers who had not experienced advancement where they worked (and who thus presumably have become more entrenched in their jobs than promoted workers) said they would be reluctant to move away from their community. These reluctant workers included both those who said they would feel "bad" about moving and those who said it would "depend on where." Only 38 percent of the workers who had experienced advancement were reluctant to move to a new neighborhood.

10

COMMUNITY PROTEST AND THE WORKING POOR

In the summer of 1967, Detroit made national headlines and achieved a new image for itself, though not a very enviable one. The city was the scene of the most destructive riot ever to occur in the United States. More than 40 people were killed, thousands were injured, thousands more were arrested, and property damage surpassed 250 million dollars.

During the same summer, Newark, New Haven, and dozens of other cities were also shattered by major riots of a racial character. *Newsweek* described the epidemic: "In Southbend, Indiana—gunfire, fire bombing and stone throwing. In Cambridge, Maryland—arson and destruction. In Toledo, Ohio—bricks and bottles. In Chicago—looting and Molotov cocktails. In Sacramento, Los Angeles—bombing. In Milwaukee—demonstrations, hatred, and violence."[1]

Similar riots, pitting whites against blacks, have not been uncommon in the United States. Before and after the summer of 1967 open manifestations of urban unrest and community protest have occurred on a fairly regular basis. In this chapter, the focus is on such occurrences and the role played in them by ghetto residents employed in unskilled, dead–end jobs.

Profile of Community Protest

The ghetto riots of the late 1960's received much attention. Concern focused upon their causes and consequences, as well as on what constitutes a riot. One description follows:

> Regardless of the reason for violence . . . riotous actions can be extremely destructive. Such actions may consist of indiscriminate looting and burning or open attacks on officials, buildings, and innocent passers-by. Rioters are limited in their actions only by their ingenuity, the training of their leaders, and the weapons, supplies, equipment, and materials available to them. The degree of violence will depend upon a number of factors, such as type and number of persons involved, location, cause of disturbance, and weapons available.[2]

This description of riots is written in such cold, dispassionate terms that it sounds as if it comes from an army manual. In fact it does. It was included as part of an army field manual released in March 1968 entitled *Civil Disturbances and Disasters*. The manual was prepared to help army personnel in coping with rioters when called to the scene to assist local police.

In *Understanding the Negro Protest,* black writer Heacock traces the various types of opposition demonstrations that have been recorded in American history. He arrives at the conclusion that demonstrations and protests are "an American tradition."[3] Commenting on one type of demonstration that has been particularly common, Heacock notes, "The strike, for example, is a form of demonstration—a remonstrance against what is considered an intolerable condition."[4] Many civil rights activists, including H. Rap Brown, have similarly looked at the tradition of protest in the United States. "Violence is as American as apple pie," Brown once commented.[5]

The race riots of the last decade were labeled by some as the work of foreign agents intent on undermining the United States. But others closer to the scene knew better, and most of the evidence ultimately proved to be on their side. One of these close observers commented: "The riots in the city streets are not the work of sinister communist agents, except where such agents move in to exploit an already festering situation. Nor are they the work of hoodlums bent on the destruction of the fruits of years of patient and interracial effort. They are the social expressions of pent–up anxiety and frustration which derive from the hopelessness of the conditions under which those people live."[6]

The features of the riots and the factors responsible for them have indeed been widely discussed. Heacock gave this interpretation:

> You must understand our mood today, if you would understand why we are in the streets. We are in the streets because we are all tight inside, and that tightness is compounded of many things: Our history in this land proclaimed as freedom land, our frustration and our anger, our anguish and suffering, our sometimes wavering sometimes almost psychogenic belief in the dreams and ideals of democracy.[7]

Black psychologist Kenneth Clark also expressed his view on the subject. Arguing that the riots were to be expected, he noted that people confined to black urban ghettos comprise "a depressed, alienated and finally destructive urban underclass."[8] This group, according to Clark, has had continuous contact with violence of one sort or another. "The chronic riot of their day to day lives," he states, "is, as far as they're concerned, no worse than the acute riots . . . They don't have anything to lose, including their lives. It's not just desperation—it's what–the–hell."[9]

A similar interpretation is provided by Dick Gregory. He notes that in addition to the frequent physical violence that is directed at blacks, the black person faces each day "violence to his human dignity." Gregory further comments:

> He learns the violence of being told he cannot go to good schools, and then being told he cannot get a good job because he hasn't been to a good school, then again being told that he can't go to a good hotel or restaurant because he hasn't the money, or the clothes or the manners the other two would have given him. . . . It is a violent reminder to the Negro in the ghetto that he may not still be a slave, but he is yet a serf, indentured to the land.[10]

In reviewing the interpretive comments of riot observers and participants a consensus of opinion emerges that one of the causes of riots is a deep–seated desire on the part of ghetto blacks to lash out at white society for the conditions under which they have long suffered. This reaction was clearly present in a small black child living in the ghetto when he commented to his mother after viewing the spectacle of police being fought and of white–owned property being destroyed: "I figured the whole world might get changed around. I figured people would treat us better from now on."[11]

Many observers believe that riots are more than spontaneous, emotional outbursts on the part of long discontented ghetto inhabitants; that they are conscious efforts to bring attention to the intolerable state of affairs that exists in the ghetto in the hope that help will follow. Still others feel that riots are often aimed at frightening whites into treating blacks better. According to Dick Gregory, white society inadvertently encouraged many blacks to love Malcolm X. He explains: "Martin Luther King said, 'love your fellow man and turn the other cheek,' and he was called a nigger and a communist and thrown in jail. Malcolm X said, 'get a gun and defend yourself, the pink–eyed devils need to be dead.' He was not arrested nor was he thrown in jail, because America respects the man with a gun."[12]

The point of view that those involved in riots are often acting in the hope that they can coerce white society into dealing with their problems more seriously is supported by the fact that riots often have had this end result. Again Dick Gregory is a firm believer that the riots have helped break the pattern of government refusal to listen to demands of ghetto residents. He gives examples to support his view.

The summer riot season in Chicago in 1966 began in the Puerto Rican neighborhood. Many people in Chicago have always wondered why there were no Puerto Rican cops. The official answer from city hall has been, "we don't have anything against Puerto Ricans, but the official height standard for Chicago policemen

is five feet, ten inches. Puerto Ricans are just too short." If
Puerto Rican leaders go to city hall and ask that the height requirements be lowered three inches to allow more Puerto Ricans
to become policemen, they will be politely but firmly refused.
After the Puerto Ricans threw bricks in their neighborhood for
three days, the height requirement was lowered three inches—
an inch per day of rioting. If the riots had lasted a month, there
would be job openings on the Chicago police force for Spanish-
speaking midgets.[13]

Negro leaders had been politely asking city hall for some swimming pools. And city hall turned a deaf ear to them. So the
residents of the ghetto decided to create their own swimming
pools by turning on the fire hydrants. When the cops came to
shut the hydrants off, the trouble started. It seems strange to
me that white folks should want to turn off the water in a
colored neighborhood. They have been trying to run away from
hot nigger stink for a hundred years. Instead of turning off the
water, they should have brought in some soap. Since the bricks
were thrown all over the west side of Chicago, it is hard now to
walk in that section without stepping into a swimming pool. The
government conveniently found the 40 million dollars after the
rioting which did not seem to be available before. It was the
same pattern in Los Angeles. Before the rioting, few people had
ever heard of the Watts section of Los Angeles. After the bricks
were thrown, some 200 million dollars were poured into that
community in emergency funds.[14]

Community Protest in Three Cities

Eight months prior to the riot in Newark in the summer
of 1967 that became the second worst in the nation during that
destructive year, a book entitled *Newark* was published.
"Newark through the summer of 1966," wrote the author,
"had not been rocked by the riots and disorder that had swept
other cities. It certainly is not a matter of luck. For one thing,
there long has been sincere dialogue between volunteer Negro
and white leaders. City–appointed racially mixed commissions
have worked hard at settling racial tensions before the point
of explosion."[15] The writer undoubtedly regretted his words
on July 14, 1967, the day that Newark exploded in open
black rebellion.

Nathan Wright was on the scene when the riot began. He describes what he saw:

We parked our car alongside the Fidelity Union Trust Company branch building on the southwest corner of the intersection. Before I could get out, we heard a loud thud and the ringing of broken glass. At the northwest corner of the intersection a liquor store front had been broken through.

Barbara [his wife] urged that we leave. I promised we would in a moment. Barbara and Bunky [his 17-year-old daughter] locked themselves in the car and I stepped onto the sidewalk adjacent to the Fidelity Union Trust.

Almost immediately there was chaos. The liquor store was ransacked. Men ran by with bottles of liquor in their hands and under their arms. The intersection swarmed with people coming suddenly out of nowhere. With the sound of thunder, the large plate glass window of the bank, just a few feet from our car was broken. . . .

There was the sound of broken glass as someone threw a bottle into the street. It landed several hundred yards away from the intersection. One of the three policemen near the intersection searched into a patrol car and pulled out a rifle. He fired up into the buildings in several directions.[16]

According to Tom Hayden, who wrote a book about the riot entitled *Rebellion in Newark,* more than 3,000 people were arrested, injured, or killed in Newark. The exact circumstances that triggered the Newark riot are still unclear. It seems that the black community learned that a black cab driver had been arrested and, according to eyewitnesses, mistreated by a white policeman. But as Wright pointed out, "For those in the bleak streets of Newark's black communities, the precise details of the report of police mistreatment was of no major concern. Repressions, abuse, and a seeming disregard for the dignity and life of persons reflect a pervasive pattern in central city life."[17]

Wright detailed a series of incidents in the preceding winter and spring that he believed helped bring the riot about. There was a controversy over the location of a medical–dental school in Newark in which the desire of the black community was disregarded. Another controversy in which the wishes of the black community were pushed aside concerned the selection of an administrator of the Newark Board of Education. Wright described what happened:

> In May, 1967 City Hall sources announced that one James Callaghan, a former student at St. Aloysius High School who later received a high school equivalency certificate by studying at night, was to be named Secretary to the Board of Education. The position of Secretary to the Board of Education is most crucial to the city's schools. He is accounting officer for the budget of the schools and is chief administrator for the official work of the Board of Education. Also contending for the position of Secretary to the Board of Education was a young black certified public accountant, Wilbur Parker. Mr. Parker is the holder of both a Bachelor's and a Master's degree from Cornell, the latter degree in business administration. Newspapers editorialized in his favor. Protest meetings were held. Businessmen and religious leaders spoke their support of the black community's desire that a highly qualified man, who was also a Negro, occupy the most critical position affecting a school system that is 80 percent black.[18]

After the Newark riot began, its duration and intensity was apparently increased due to improper handling of the situation by local police and soldiers brought in to assist. Hayden gave his observations of the reactions of the soldiers:

> Because of racism, the troops are unfamiliar with both the people and the structure of the ghetto. Patrol duty after dark becomes a frightening and exhausting experience, especially for men who want to return alive to their families and homes. A psychology of desperation leads to careless and indiscriminate violence toward the community, including reprisal killing, which inflames the people whom the troops were sent to pacify.[19]

Previous riots have been recorded in Newark, although the earliest ones were not of a racial character. The first disturbance on record took place in 1745 amid circumstances not unlike those of the 1967 riot. Newark historian John T. Cunningham described how on September 19 of that year the city "exploded in mid–afternoon when a band of 150 men came into town with clubs, axes, and crowbars." The group was intent on freeing from jail a friend who they believed had been improperly arrested. "The mob paused only long enough to warn the sheriff that if anyone should be arrested for the caper, they would return 'with double the number of men' and might even bring a hundred Indians to help."[20]

At the time of the Civil War, another disturbance took place in Newark. This occurred, according to Cunningham, after President Lincoln announced a draft of able–bodied young men. Community leaders were successful in persuading people to emulate the protest riots that were occurring in New York.

The riots in Baltimore and Cleveland during the epidemic of the late 1960's were less substantial than the Newark disturbance. In 1968 several Cleveland policemen who were repairing a police vehicle in a black community were fired upon and killed by black snipers perched on roof tops. The next few days brought in additional police and saw widespread looting and violence. The riot would have been far worse if it had not been for the foresight of Cleveland's black mayor, Carl Stokes, who gave strict instructions to police so that their actions would not aggravate the situation.

The biggest riot in Baltimore also occurred in 1968. Although, as in other major cities, predictions had been made of a riot, it was expected to take place during the summer. Instead, it occurred earlier, immediately following the assassination of Martin Luther King on April 5. The following day brought widespread disorder in Baltimore, at the same time that near–by Washington erupted in violence. The toll of the Baltimore riot was estimated at 6 killed, 600 injured, 1,200 fires, and 1,100 businesses damaged by fire, vandalism, and looting. Property damage was estimated to be 13.5 million dollars.[21]

Similar to other U.S. cities, the riot in Baltimore was not the first incident of this type in the city. On October 2, 1919, a newspaper article described a disturbance:

> Trouble between several hundred soldiers and Negroes in which shots were fired and sticks and stones hurled were checked by police after six arrests had been made. The trouble started when a bottle was thrown at four infantry men who had gathered a group of 200 soldiers and tried to terrorize the neighborhood.[22]

Work Discontent and Community Protest

Following the destructive riots of 1967, President Johnson established a commission to investigate the disturbances. The commission collected substantial data on the participants and the circumstances surrounding their participation. It found that the rioters were mainly people employed in low–level jobs rather than those without work. The Commission's report said: "In the riot cities which we surveyed, Negroes were three times as likely as whites to hold unskilled jobs, which are often part–time, seasonal, low–paying, and 'dead–end'—a fact that creates a problem for Negroes as significant as unemployment."[23]

At Congressional hearings that followed the release of the Commission's report, many noted authorities appeared and expressed their view that the confinement of blacks to menial jobs poses a serious threat to society. They predicted periodic riots in the future unless something was done to significantly alter this employment situation. After listening to many speakers, Congressman Richard Bolling of Missouri commented: "Several witnesses have mentioned the number underemployed, which we do not seem to deal very well with at this level of the Congress—we do not seem to understand the implications of underemployment. Underemployment may be even worse in some respects than unemployment."[24]

The fact that the typical rioter was found by the Riot Commission to be a discontented worker should not have come as surprise to anyone. Throughout history disgruntled workers have been the foremost participants in protest actions and rebellions. During the 1950's in Cuba, for example, revolutionary leader Fidel Castro found his supporters to be "five–hundred thousand farm laborers inhabiting miserable shacks . . . sharing their misery with their children, who have not an inch of land to cultivate . . . and four–hundred thousand industrial laborers and stevedores . . . whose homes are wretched quarters, whose salaries pass from the hands of the boss to those of usurers, whose future is a pay reduction and dismissal, whose life is eternal work and whose only rest is in the tomb."[25]

Since the release of the Riot Commission's report, other studies of the riots have appeared. One, sponsored by the Office of Law Enforcement Assistance of the United States Department of Justice, was undertaken to develop a rating scale that could be used by local police officials to forecast the time and place of future riots. It is significant that the scale developed included a job dissatisfaction index, the study having found a definite correlation between job dissatisfaction and community protest.[26]

Facts presented in previous chapters concerning the ill effects of confinement to unskilled work on people in general, and on blacks in particular, give many clues to explain why black unskilled workers are predisposed to protest and rebellion. That black workers live in slum conditions and the hostility and hopelessness this generates is intensified by the menial jobs they hold is only one of the causes of mass protest among this population segment.

The riots have spurred extensive study of the phenomenon of violence. One compilation reports the conclusions of several studies on the subject. Many experts, it is noted, believe that violence comes naturally to all human beings.[27] Citing Freud's theory that aggression and destruction are basic human instincts, it is argued that society must provide outlets for people to channel these tendencies. The major outlet, agree the experts, is work. "In varying degrees," comments one writer, "work offers an outlet—probably one of the most useful outlets—for the hostile, aggressive drive which is a major source of psychic energy."[28] Those who hold this view are quick to point out that "some types of occupations do not in themselves offer a sufficient outlet for this aggressive energy."[29] They note that only if work provides the opportunity for a person to fully express himself, to realize his potential, and to exert some control over his functions does it constitute such an outlet.

Unskilled jobs do not provide these opportunities. At the same time, they have features that actually appear to foster tendencies toward violence, such as boredom and monotony. According to an article entitled "The Bored and the Violent," these stimulate violence, particularly that without a clearly defined purpose.[30] The indiscriminate violence involved in riots is of this type.

One of the witnesses at the congressional hearings, Vivian W. Henderson, President of black Clark College, also argued the relationship between boredom and violence. "As my teacher used to tell me, the idle brain is the devil's workshop. I think some of the problems we have in the cities and some of the tension that is in the rural areas suggest to me that we ought to begin to think about the consequences of an idle brain and an idle person."[31] Along these lines, John Scott wrote about ways of avoiding future violence and disorder. He recommended that "we need to provide young adult males with useful, constructive, and rewarding activities. . . ."[32]

Even if violence is not a natural human instinct, there are many things about unskilled, dead–end jobs that can lead people to it. A storehouse of frustration and anguish is built up by unskilled black workers as a result of their jobs, while at the same time they are prevented from obtaining satisfactory compensation after hours. Trapped simultaneously in menial jobs and the ghetto, they are likely to be extremely resentful and will express their resentment through some form of rebellious behavior, often physical.

The holders of a menial, monotonous job are likely to rebel with physical force because their job has conditioned them to act physically and spontaneously rather than through purposive, thoughtful action. The work experience fosters an ambivalence resulting from the economic and social pressures that compel them to work, on the one hand, and their dislike for the job, on the other. Studies have found that ambivalent attitudes are very conducive to group protest,[33] as is the aimless and nondirective orientation characterizing unskilled workers. The latter makes it difficult for them to become effectively organized in the community and gives them a distrust for leaders. For the only leaders they know on the job are usually completely authoritarian and nonresponsive to their feelings. Thus, notes Kenneth Clark, "The prisoners of the ghetto riot without reason, without organization, and without leadership, as this is generally understood. The rioting is in itself a repudiation of leadership. It is the expression of the anarchy of the profoundly alienated."[34]

Another feature of unskilled work conducive to violence and open protest is the feeling of powerlessness it induces. An earlier chapter discussed this in considering why unskilled black workers do not participate in social and political institutions in traditionally accepted ways. The relationship between powerlessness and violence was revealed in the Riot Commission report: "The frustrations of powerlessness have led some Negroes to the conviction that there is no effective alternative to violence as a means of achieving redress of grievances and of 'moving the system.' "[35]

Even though most of the damage is often done to their own communities, the acts of black group disorder are often attempts to punish whites. Confinement to unrewarding jobs appears to contribute to this form of black racism. Blacks holding menial jobs experience prejudice, discrimination, and inequality in the work setting which reinforces their experiences on the outside. The result, as one study found, is that "the militant Negro is particularly common among blue–collar workers found in large urban ghettos."[36]

Since some of the most blatant forms of discrimination are practiced in the work setting, many blacks who might previously have only disliked whites because of isolated incidents of discrimination become extremely hostile after working closely with them for some time. This is often enough to push many blacks who have long entertained the thought of "striking back" to the point of actually doing so. As one writer has commented, "People who are spat upon continually sooner or later rebel."[37]

Color consciousness among blacks manifests itself at work through competition for the few higher level jobs that become available to unskilled workers. The fact that this competitive situation "promotes racial tension and conflict" was brought out in a study of interaction between white and black workers.[38] Another study on the same subject detected a "rising tension within the plant among those long employed but rarely advanced. . . ."[39]

Robert C. Weaver, in a survey of companies that were forced by the labor shortage during World War II to open their doors for the first time to black workers, found substantial mutual hostility between whites and blacks. He explained the reaction of whites to their black coworkers as follows: "The entry of the Negro into new spheres of activity brought the 'race problem' into the experience of hundreds of thousands of Americans who never before had any real contact with it. . . . Most of them accepted the popular misconceptions about race. . . ."[40]

If it is true that entrapment in menial jobs has played a role in causing ghetto residents to rebel through the mode of physical violence, the question of why such rebellion takes place away from the job rather than on it must be answered. Since most unskilled positions are carefully supervised, the opportunity to deviate and rebel simply does not exist, at least not more than once. There is evidence that when holders of menial jobs have the opportunity to engage in defiant, rebellious behavior on the job, they will take full advantage. The story is told of a discontented railroad car loader who often worked unsupervised. "No parcel was safe in his hands. Those marked 'fragile' were open invitations to him to hurl and kick them into the car."[41] Another case of on–the–job deviancy was observed in unskilled workers left alone in a paper mill: "It may comfort the fashionable ladies who insist upon having their parcels wrapped to know that the paper was freshly impregnated with urine."[42]

But for most workers in unskilled jobs, close and constant supervision prevents them from venting their resentment and hostility at its source. This must wait until they leave the work setting. Dick Gregory, in discussing the negative image black ghetto residents have of policemen, said, "The cop is as close as the man in the ghtto can get to the system which oppresses him."[43] For discontented black workers, the policeman may well be looked upon as a substitute for a hated white supervisor or company owner.

Unlike low–level white workers, who are able to move into any of a number of white communities and live there among people with various occupations and life situations, black workers are confined largely to the few communities that white society has designated for them. They are concentrated together with all of their frustrations, dissatisfactions, and hostilities. In this situation, the predisposition toward open protest is found in more than a few people—it is a community–wide tendency. Recognizing this, Kenneth Clark has noted: "It is no longer possible to confine hundreds of thousands of uneducated, underemployed, purposeless young people and adults . . . without storing up social dynamite."[44]

Contrary to popular opinion, black ghetto residents employed in menial jobs do not see themselves as better off than their unemployed neighbors. There is a logical explanation for this. A sociologist who has studied revolutionary movements has pointed out that people must expect an improvement in their condition before participating in a rebellion. He writes: "It is the dissatisfied state of mind rather than the tangible position of 'adequate' or 'inadequate' supply of food, equality, or liberty, which produces revolution."[45] Another writer, applying this theory to urban unrest in America, states: "The Negroes' impatience, bitterness, and anger . . . are likely to increase the closer they come to full equality. . . . Indeed, it is a commonplace of history that revolutions stem from hope, not despair; from progress, not stalemate. And the nearer to triumph the revolutionaries get, the tougher they usually become."[46]

It is therefore likely that placing unemployed blacks in unskilled jobs will not pacify them. It may very well have the opposite affect. In *Oakland's Not for Burning,* author Amory Bradford points out, "It would not be realistic for the white community to expect protest to subside in the face of gains, for the closer the Negro community gets to the attainment of its goal—the removal of the causes and effects of racial exploitation and powerlessness—the more impatient will Negroes become for full equality."[47] Most unskilled employed blacks who participated in the riots expressed the same view when interviewed by the Riot Commission. Their standard complaint was their menial jobs. They all said they wanted "jobs with dignity."[48] This pattern prompted the Riot Commission to recommend that employment for a ghetto resident "must not appear to the hard–core person to be a dead–end job. . . . It must be made clear to him from the outset that his satisfactory performance at the entry level will result not only in continued employment after the training period but also in an opportunity for advancement ideally through a clearly defined job ladder with step increases in both pay and responsibility."[49] Following through with this recommendation, former Secretary of Labor George Schultz announced a program "to help employers train low–level workers for more demanding tasks." In making the announcement, Schultz commented that one of the goals of the program was to relieve "tensions increasingly associated in our society with routine, low–paying work."[50]

Attitudes Toward Community Protest: Survey Results

Although the Riot Commission study showed that unskilled blacks employed in low–level jobs comprise the majority of rioters, the survey conducted by this author covering attitudes of unskilled and paraprofessional black workers disclosed that the higher–level workers take a more positive view of rioting. Of the paraprofessionals interviewed, 69 percent felt that after a riot the government tries harder to help a ghetto community, while 55 percent of the unskilled workers held this view. A greater proportion of unskilled workers than paraprofessionals regarded riots as having unfavorable consequences. The majority (54%) of the unskilled considered the effects of riots to be negative and only 23 percent viewed the effects as' positive. In contrast, only 41 percent of the paraprofessionals felt that a riot has negative consequences, while 47 percent saw the effects as positive. Many unskilled workers made comments about the aftermath of riots such as, "They don't make no improvements" and "The neighborhood completely deteriorates."

If unskilled workers take such a negative view of rioting, why are they the ones to engage in it and not the higher-level workers who seem to feel that its effects are beneficial? In order to answer this, one must consider the psychology of the riot participant. As revealed previously, paraprofessionals are more discontented with living in the ghetto than unskilled workers. The unskilled worker, meanwhile, is more discontented with his job. The fact that both are discontented, yet one group openly rebels and the other does not, may be due to the strong influence the job has on unskilled workers. A menial, dead–end job is very frustrating and not likely to provide a suitable outlet for aggression and hostility. It is also likely to create feelings of powerlessness, making the expression of grievances through physical means, rather than through conventional social or political channels, seem more appropriate. Also, black workers confined to menial jobs frequently experience prejudice and are therefore more likely to want to strike back at whites.

It should also be remembered, as previously pointed out, that the paraprofessionals interviewed were concerned with more long-range, abstract goals than the unskilled workers, who tended to focus on immediate needs. This helps to explain the apparent contradiction between the unskilled workers' feelings about the effects of riots and their actual participation in them. Confinement to menial work creates attitudes of ambivalence among workers, which leads to the aimless destructiveness characterizing riots. The rioters strike out destructively without any abstract purpose in mind. Their concern is with their immediate needs, whether to let out the aggression which is pent up on the job or to acquire a TV set. Simply stated, unskilled workers do not view riots as being constructive, because they do not mean to be. They are not trying to improve the community by their behavior. The paraprofessional, however, sees the riots as constructive, probably because they view their effects in terms of long-range ideological goals. But since the beneficial effects of a riot may have on the community are not immediate, they are too abstract for unskilled workers to be concerned with in view of their immediate priorities.

Yet the higher-level workers usually do not participate in open community rebellion. This too seems to result from the influence of their jobs. In contrast to bottom–level workers, their work is less frustrating, less physical, has more personal meaning, and serves as a better outlet for aggressive feelings. The paraprofessionals were found to have a higher incidence of voting. This indicates that they express their discontent more often through acceptable channels. It is therefore understandable that they are less likely to take part in illegal acts of protest.

From the survey data collected, an analysis was performed to determine whether there was a correlation between experiences on the job and attitudes toward riots. One interesting finding was revealed by responses to the question of what workers think happens to a community that has had a riot. An equal proportion of promoted and nonpromoted workers (about 60%) felt that the government tries harder to help a community after a riot. Yet, interestingly, fewer workers who have experienced a promotion felt that "nothing changes one way or the other" as compared to workers who have not had a promotion. The figures are 14 percent and 25 percent, respectively. The conclusion may be drawn from this that workers who have experienced occupational mobility are more change–oriented in matters away from work than other workers. Since they have seen that their own job status was capable of being changed, they are more likely to view things away from work as subject to alteration.

Another interesting finding was that black workers who had jobs that made them feel like a "somebody" favored harsher treatment of rioters than workers who felt like a "nobody." In the "somebody" group 84 percent believed that people arrested in riots should definitely be punished, compared with a lesser proportion (71%) of "nobody" workers. This finding may appear somewhat contradictory in view of the finding that the paraprofessionals comprised most of the workers who felt like a "somebody," and that these higher–level workers considered the effects of riots to be positive. The present finding indicates simply that while they view the end result of a riot as favorable, they do not approve of the method. This further explains why higher–level workers do not participate in riots. Since they favor traditional channels to bring about reform and condemn illegal methods of protest, it is to be expected that they would punish those who use such illegal methods.

Since unskilled workers, the "nobodies," usually are the ones involved in rioting, they logically would recommend leniency for those arrested. It should be noted, however, that the majority of workers in both groups favor punishment for the arrested. Both categories seem to feel that a jail sentence of up to thirty days, or between one month and a year, is the most appropriate punishment.

11

THE PROBLEM IN PERSPECTIVE

In the previous chapters the problem of the confinement of blacks to unskilled, dead–end jobs was considered and its consequences were explored. The holders of such jobs were seen to be in a situation in which many adverse influences are exerted on their psychological, social, and economic well–being. Blacks were found to be particularly susceptible to the detrimental consequences of confinement to menial work.

At the outset the overall meaning of work in society was considered. The conclusion was reached that work is an important concern both to society and to its individual members. A person derives many things from his job, economic support being only one. Following this discussion of the social, psychological, and economic significance of work, attention was directed to low–level jobs. Considered were the features of these jobs and the people who typically hold them. These jobs were found to be boring, low–paying, and dead–end. They involve simple, repetitive tasks that call for little thought or self–initiative. The poverty wages paid to those performing them led to the use of the term "working poor" to describe this group of people. The typical holders of these jobs were found to be blacks living in city ghettos. A large proportion of blacks are confined to bottom–level jobs for several reasons, racial discrimination of one type or another being the foremost.

Since blacks were found to be the typical unskilled job-holders, a background discussion was provided on the cultural heritage and present status of blacks in America before considering the reaction of black workers to confinement to menial jobs. The topics covered in this discussion ranged from the many forms of discrimination aimed at blacks to conditions in the contemporary black ghetto. Detailed attention was then given to the reaction of unskilled black workers to their low–level jobs. Previous research was utilized in drawing conclusions about the psychological and emotional impact of these jobs on black workers. The results of a special survey, conducted by the author, of the attitudes and perceptions of black workers were also presented. The survey revealed that low–level jobs give workers few skills, poverty wages, and little personal satisfaction. Workers were found to advance rarely. Many did not even try because they felt that discrimination blocked the path to promotion. After reviewing the evidence, the conclusion was reached that the psychological adjustment of black workers is adversely affected by their experience in low–level jobs. The historical background and contemporary situation of blacks were found to be largely responsible for their particularly negative reaction to low–skill, dead–end work.

To further understand the implications of confinement to menial jobs for this group of people, their after–work lives were studied. The family life and social relations of blacks in unskilled jobs were compared to those of blacks in higher–level positions. It was found that both family life and social relations were adversely affected by the work experiences of unskilled blacks. This indicated that the consequences of menial work for blacks go beyond the work setting. It was learned that these black workers greatly desired a gratifying home and social life as compensation for the gratification denied them in their work.

The after–work consequences of confinement to menial jobs were further explored by considering the political attitudes and voting behavior of unskilled black workers. A strong relationship was found between political involvement and occupational status. Black persons in menial jobs, in contrast to higher–level black workers, tend to steer away from most forms of political involvement and are apathetic about public issues. It was found that their jobs produce feelings of power-lessness and ambivalence which are responsible for their alienated political posture.

The ghetto conditions in which unskilled black workers live were also considered. An effort was made to determine the possible influence of menial jobs on the adjustment of blacks to these conditions. It was found that holding a low–skill, low–wage job increases dissatisfaction with impoverished living conditions. The confinement of ghetto blacks to menial jobs also serves to convince them that their confinement to the ghetto will be permanent.

Finally, the topic of urban unrest and community protest within the black ghetto was considered, with emphasis on the role that black ghetto residents employed in low–level jobs play in incidents of group protest. The findings of the National Commission on Civil Disorders on the riots of the late 1960's were presented, notably the fact that the typical rioter in the ghetto is not unemployed but rather a discontented, unskilled employed worker. Evidence from the survey conducted by the author supported this finding.

Understanding the Problem

The detrimental effects on blacks of being trapped in menial jobs are many. Most obviously, these individuals ex-perience severe economic hardship. Thus the term "working poor" has been adopted to refer to them. Many of these people would actually be better off, from an economic standpoint, if they went on welfare. They might be better off from other standpoints, as it was found that confinement to menial jobs can have ill effects on the psychological well–being and after–

work lives of people and was conducive to the recent rash of urban violence and mass disorder.

At the Riot Commission hearings that followed the release of the Commission's report in 1968, Berkely Burrell, President of the National Business League, said:

> The fact is that in 1968 merely a "useful job" is not enough to "fully utilize the human resources" we are talking about. The committee must accelerate its redefinition of public policy about "employment" to mean "employment in upwardly mobile careers" and "employment as potential managers in businesses that provide access to a stake in the capital accumulation system." That is where the action is in American society and unless the black man obtains the opportunity to qualify there, unless he obtains access to the wherewithals to compete in business, et cetera, not just equal job opportunity but access to equal participation in business, we will still be imposing on black men the subtle steel net of slavery, an advanced form of it to be sure, but one in which he is still but the instrument in the hands of another and not "his own man."[1]

Recent government recognition of the problem of captivity of black workers in menial jobs is indicated by the introduction of such new terms in government reports as "under–employment," "subemployment," and "underutilization." These terms refer to the fact that the majority of the working poor are employed in occupations below their highest skill or functioning below their present capacity or below their potential if they had more education or training. Urban Leaguer Midgett Parker, an innovator of quality employment programs, has a term of his own to describe these categories of workers: "slave labor of the 1970's."

A government report recognizing the existence of the problem, though making few suggestions for solving it, said: "With the lessening unemployment problem in the past few years, the other forms of underutilization of manpower have come into clearer view."[2] Another report used the term of subemployment, commenting: "The concept of subemployment reflects the judgment that workers with low earnings may have problems of as much concern from the viewpoint of manpower policy as those of many workers with substantial unemployment."[3]

Also not to be overlooked is the fact that the problem of underemployment is related to that of unemployment. For one thing, the prospect of working hard in a job that offers little in rewards and promises to lead nowhere discourages many unskilled people from seeking work. In addition, the fact that people in low–level jobs rarely move upward means that their jobs do not become available to the unemployed. Commenting on underemployment, Nathan Wright has said: "Until all people in our cities have a sense that they have worth as persons, until they are educated toward the realization of their very best capacities, the cities cannot possibly avoid continuing unrest."[4] Blacks with low–level jobs have "stunted lives."[5]

That minority discontent and resulting social upheavals are partially a product of the black man's disappointment at not being able to get a good job stems from the American expectation that everyone will strive for success. Similarly, as described by a historian, Luther defected from the Roman Catholic church in response to its teachings: "Luther's revolt against the Medieval church arose from a desperate effort to follow the way by her prescribed. Luther responded to his church upbringing so intensely that he became permeated with a sense of deep unworthiness and with intolerable feelings of guilt."[6]

Many people who have observed the far–ranging implications of the existence of the working poor have argued that although training the unskilled for higher level work, providing follow–up counseling services, and creating a more favorable job market will cost money, the costs to society are likely to be much greater if the unused energies and talents of these people are directed at striking back at society. "Not to incorporate an alienated individual into the mainstream of society" comments one social analyst, "will be more costly than the $7,025 spent per job corps enrollee or the $900 to $1,000 spent per MTDA (Manpower Training and Development Act) trainee. The cost of confining a man to prison for 10 years, for maintaining his wife and four children, is far greater."[7]

The problem is not solving itself, if anything, it is getting worse. In 1970 the Equal Employment Opportunity Commission released the findings of a comprehensive national survey of the percentages of white and black workers in various occupational categories. It found that "the nonwhite percentages in the better–paying jobs are even lower than had been expected."[8] A large percentage of black workers were found in such low–skill jobs as laborer, while in higher–level occupations, such as the mechanical trades, only a handful of blacks were counted. Commenting on the Commission's findings, Chairman William H. Brown said that the study revealed to him that "the pervasive pattern in all American industry is the inverse relationship between pay and skill level and minority group employment."[9]

For a final commentary, NAACP labor director Herbert Hill, speaking at a government hearing, is quoted:

> Sure there's been progress. Compared to where we were at the time of Emancipation, I suppose there is great progress! Or in terms of where the Negro was in the Post-Reconstruction period, there's great progress! Or where we were in terms of the condition of the American Negro during the Great Depression of the 1930's, there is great progress! But the only realistic measure of progress is what is the status of Negroes in relation to the status of other groups in the society. That is the only meaningful criterion.[10]

Toward A Solution

The first step in solving the problem of the black working poor is to fully acknowledge its existence. This is what Vivian Henderson, President of black Clark College, recommended when he stood up at the Riot Commission hearing and said:

> All I am pleading for is that we get rid of the myth that we have only to deal with the hard-core unemployed; there is a problem here but they constitute a minor part of the problem. The heart of the problem is with the marginal workers, those in and out

of the labor force, and those on the fringes. We need to devote more attention to these people.[11]

Understanding that the problem is distinct from the unemployment problem, and far more complex, it is apparent that the solution is not simply to provide more welfare money to live on. Shortsighted solutions of this type may be similar to throwing gasoline on a fire to put it out. As far as providing more jobs is concerned, the emphasis must be on quality employment. And regarding the need for people to obtain a living income, the need is not simply to hand out money to them, but to provide a personally rewarding way of earning it.

One shortsighted solution to the problem was attacked by Max Lerner. He said:

> It has become a truism to say that everything will fall into place if only the Negro poor have a decent income, and there is enough truth in this to make the battle for something like a guaranteed family income a valid one. Yet income alone, or even a job alone, is not enough. It must be work rather than a job, putting back into the work concept some of the pride and sense of vocation that the Protestant ethic gave it and that, perhaps, the Negro has moved furthest from. When Ralph Abernathy organized a "poor people's march" on Washington, he defined the objective thus: "To plague the Pharaohs of this nation with plague after plague until they agree to give us meaningful jobs and a guaranteed annual income."[12]

At the Riot Commission hearing on employment prob-lems a good deal of the initial talk centered on the need to provide black ghetto residents with more jobs, regardless of what types they might be. Recognizing the danger of this limited approach, many manpower experts present at the hearing raised their voices in protest. Professor Eli Ginzberg was one of those present who expressed concern. He said, "We are in a very difficult dilemma, because many Negroes, in my opinion are not talking about jobs—they are talking about jobs with a future."[13]

The needs of unskilled blacks are not simply for jobs that will occupy their time and give them wages and steady work, but rather jobs that will be personally rewarding to them and which will help them develop their potential. It has been found that when black ghetto residents are given the choice of interesting work over steady work, they will invariably choose the interesting work.[14] Nor are economic considerations always the most important factors in choosing a job.

Unskilled blacks clearly have the potential to assume skilled and supervisory positions. All that is required is the proper training, the proper guidance, and the job opportunities. In some instances, the amount of training needed by unskilled blacks to assume responsible positions is far less than is commonly assumed. Reports of illegal activities in the black ghetto clearly indicate that many "unskilled" blacks involved in such endeavors as large–scale gambling operations have considerable business and managerial talent.

For the majority of unskilled blacks, whether presently employed or not, quality training is needed. For those employed, not only is training required to provide them with the skills they need to assume higher level positions, but also mechanisms must be established to insure their upgrading to these higher positions. One pioneer in upgrading efforts, black consultant Leonard H. Fonville, commented on the results he saw in workers who were upgraded in one of the successful training programs he had designed. "The people felt they were no longer simply running machines, but running their own lives," Fonville reported.[15]

The mandate for government and industry is clear. Many and varied efforts must be made to attack the problem of confinement of a large number of people to low–wage, low–skill jobs that have no future except the promise of continued economic, social, and psychological impoverishment.

12

A PLAN FOR GOVERNMENT

A Matter of Priorities

There are many actions that the government can take to help workers confined to low–wage, low–skill jobs. Government officials must, as they have so far failed to do, fully appreciate the existence, complexity, and magnitude of the problem, including the fact that confinement to menial jobs can create problem individuals, which in turn can lead to problem communities.

The lack of full awareness of the problem is evident in the fact that government's employment priority has traditionally been with reducing unemployment. Year after year programs are launched aimed at bringing people into jobs, any jobs. These efforts, at best, have done nothing to solve the problem of the working poor, and, at worst, have served to aggravate it. Government campaigns to place the unemployed in summer jobs or the military service, for example, have only served to raise job expectations that are often never realized. It has been observed that unskilled workers who have undergone military training will use the techniques of violence they have learned if they rebel.[1]

Nathan Wright has discussed the many job training programs made available to the unskilled. He feels that they have suffered from deficiencies reflecting the government's non-recognition of the existence of the working poor. "Whenever black people are trained," Wright comments, "they are trained largely for frustration."[2] He feels that the greatest oversight is limiting efforts to placing people in any types of jobs. "To prepare the poor . . . for marginal, marketable skills," Wright states, "will not close the hitherto unclosing economic gap. In many ways any efforts at training for those ripe for exploitation is preparation for further frustration."[3] He recommends that the government strive for "human growth and fulfillment as its number one employment goal."[4]

Tom Hayden has observed that ghetto blacks seem to "wait observantly for the next in a lifelong series of promises to be violated."[5] He notes that one of the biggest disappointments has been the hope that government efforts at job training and placement would result in far better jobs than the bottom–level openings which have typically become available.

One example of a deficient program was a proposal to offer companies a tax rebate to create jobs. These could be expected to be "make–work" jobs, which usually turn out to be the most meaningless and intolerable of unskilled positions.

As a study found: "The problem of the poor is not lack of will to work, but is rather lack of opportunity to get the training and kind of work which will bring them a sense of achievement and a decent income."[6] Thus, underemployment can lead to unemployment, for the prospect of low–wage, low–prestige work can foster a desire not to work at all.

Many governmental manpower development efforts have concentrated on the so–called "hard–core" unemployed. This approach has little effect on the broader problem of the working poor. At the Senate hearings following the release of the Riot Commission report, Gath L. Mangum, codirector of the Center for Manpower Studies, criticized government efforts for shortsightedness. "I am interested," he said, "to see that the Commission's report focuses very heavily on recommendations for employing the hard–core unemployed, while it itself describes the typical rioter as a young Negro male having more education than his neighbors and being already employed, but employed in a menial job."[7]

It is recommended that the government refocus its efforts and concentrate on finding meaningful jobs for unskilled people, whether presently working or not. Government should recognize, as a study of the ghetto reported, "the foremost ghetto need is more jobs—steady well–paid jobs with prospects of advancement."[8] Representative James C. Corman of California was on target when he recommended to his congressional colleagues that, "We must no longer tolerate job programs which merely make work. . . ."[9]

Eliminating Discrimination

Increased efforts must be made to break down the remaining racial barriers in the placement and promotion of blacks to quality jobs. Congress has enacted many laws prohibiting most types of discrimination in hiring, training, and advancement, but they have not been rigorously enforced. This has been due less to lack of volition by public officials than to insufficient funds. It has been noted that "the total budget for the Federal, state, and municipal agencies [concerned with enforcement] is less than the advertising budget of one large concern."[10]

Greater efforts and resources for enforcement are clearly needed. Herbert Hill issued a statement after reviewing statistics showing the widespread existence of discrimination in industry: "We are forced to draw the conclusion that, law notwithstanding, executive orders notwithstanding, public policy often enunciated notwithstanding, voluntary compliance does not work!" Hill thereupon suggested that the government use the power it has as a major consumer of goods and services produced by industry to fight discrimination:

Contract cancellation is a most potent weapon, more so than the long and protracted hearings before a court of law or before a state administrative civil rights agency, and I find it absurd—in many situations the Equal Employment Opportunity Commission has found probable cause to credit the allegations of a complaint—a judge sitting in a Federal courtroom will find a union or a corporation guilty of discriminatory practices in violation of the law—a state FEPC Commission will find a union or a corporation guilty of violating the law—but they continue doing business as usual. Federal agencies, state agencies, municipal agencies continue to give them contracts, and therefore use the public tax dollars, including the tax dollars of Negro citizens, to subsidize racial discrimination.[11]

The use of government contracts as a weapon to fight discrimination has proven highly effective. Even a bigoted company president will think twice about discriminatory practices if he knows that they could result in the denial or discontinuance of a large government contract. At stake was a multibillion–dollar contract when the Defense Department in January 1970 undertook a review of employment practices at the McDonnell Douglas Corporation to determine if the firm had complied with the "fair employment provisions" which are now part of most defense contracts.

Encouraged by the success of this procedure, in September, 1969, the Federal government launched the "Philadelphia plan." It calls for racial quotas in various occupational categories to be maintained by companies in order to qualify for Federal contract. The Federal government found that in Philadelphia 40 percent of the population, but only .7 percent of the membership of the steamfitters union, was black. Since many blacks were available and qualified to become steamfitters, Federal government contracts with construction companies in the area provided that during a specified period of time black steamfitters must be increased to 20 percent or more.[12]

Job Information

In addition to eliminating discrimination, the government

should make information about jobs, especially those on a higher level, available to residents of the ghetto. It has been found that because the ghetto is a relatively self–contained community, good jobs that become available outside the area often do not become known to residents.[13] "Poor job informa· tion systems" is the technical term for this problem. The government should sponsor research and experiments to test new ways of providing job information to ghetto residents.

Buffalo, New York, has responded to this need by including an "Employment Information Center" as part of Buffalo's Model Cities program aimed at alleviating problems in its black ghettos. With a budget of almost $300,000 and a staff of 34, the center has had an impressive track record in matching residents with available job opportunities. According to Model Cities Director David Echols, the center's main function is to maintain a current inventory of job openings and training opportunities and a listing of residents available for work and/or training.[14] More than 20 "coaches" work at the center to provide personal counseling to job seekers.

A similar project, but one that takes a slightly different direction, was included in the model cities program in Fall River, Massachusetts. Paul Paulos, the director of the overall program, devised the project after seeing other antipoverty programs being staffed largely by nonresidents of the area served. He felt this was due not so much to a lack of qualified local people as to a lack of information about job openings. He therefore set up a job information center which has filled more than seven out of ten jobs in his program with local residents.

On a national scale, the United States Department of Labor has launched a project called "JOB BANK." The Job Bank consists of a sophisticated computer system in major metropolitan regions, containing computerized files of job openings in the area. According to Labor Department Regional Director Clayton J. Cottrell, an employer seeking to fill a position places a "job order" with the Job Bank.[15] Each day a computer print–out is distributed to job placement offices in the area. The print–out contains a full listing of current job openings and the qualifications sought by employers to fill the positions. This system replaces the traditional method of each job placement office maintaining a separate listing of available jobs. With the Job Bank, a master list is made available to all job placement offices, and this list is kept current on a daily basis.

The Job Bank has proven to be an effective approach, although some snags still have to be worked out. One problem is with the personnel who take the job orders, often lacking the training and sensitivity to ascertain and record the key qualifications for the jobs. Another difficulty is that the task of finding available applicants for jobs is still done manually through the use of conventional files. This often results in referrals to jobs of less than the best qualified individuals. The future refinement of the Job Bank should include a parallel "Applicant Bank" which would consist of a computer-ized file of all applicants and their qualifications. It would then be possible to match applicants to jobs much in the same way that computerized dating services purport to match in-dividuals whose characteristics show them to be compatible with each other.

Worker Upgrading Programs

Government should increase its efforts at helping menial job holders move up to better positions. The government has begun to sponsor limited programs providing in–plant training programs for low–wage, low–skill workers to enable them to acquire the skills needed for promotion. The results have been highly effective. The morale of both promoted and nonpro-moted workers seems to improve. The workers who are per-mitted to escape their dead–end jobs often improve in initiative and ambition to the point where they undertake self–help activities, such as attending night school, in an attempt to move even further up the occupational ladder. Moreover, follow–up studies show they are often successful in obtaining additional promotions. A study found that a significant number of upgraded entry–level workers were able eventually to become full–fledged professionals through their own additional efforts.[16]

In addition to sponsoring more upgrading programs, the government must continue to experiment and innovate in upgrading methods. In many companies, there is simply no job ladder that would permit low–skill workers to advance to higher level jobs, regardless of the type of training they receive. Many complex skills separate entry–level workers from the next job level. Rather than attempt to provide the lengthy training necessary for advancement to the next step, new, intermediate jobs should be created. They would involve a few of the tasks of the higher–level positions, thus providing on–the–job training that would eventually qualify workers for the higher positions themselves.

In embarking on a strategy of this type, the government could learn by looking at the techniques used in World War II when labor shortages were so severe that business was forced to find ways to put "unqualified" men and women to work in skilled jobs by reorganizing and restructuring job tasks to require less skill. For example, American optical manufacturers at the beginning of the War told Naval authorities that it was impossible to manufacture more than a few thousand prism binoculars annually, because it would take several years to train additional lens grinders. The Navy experimented, however, and soon found that it was possible to break down the lens grinding operation into several steps, thereby cutting training time to a few weeks. Enough people were brought into the trade during the war to permit the production of a half–million binoculars a year.[17]

Some government programs have clearly disregarded the problem of the working poor. For example, the state–

administered and federally–funded Employment Service offices have been criticized for their reputation of concentrating on primarily marginal, low–paying jobs. Few concerted efforts have been made by Employment Service offices to find and fill the semi–skilled and skilled jobs that exist in private industry. One of the reasons for this failing appears to be that the Employment Service is oriented more to working with job applicants rather than to serving industry. More time spent with private employers would undoubtedly lead to a greater understanding of their needs and to the possibility of developing higher quality jobs.

The government should also seek to develop new types of prestige service positions that would serve the needs of urban areas. A report recommending several new jobs of this type referred to them as "new careers,"[18] while the term paraprofessional has also been used.

One category of recommended "new careers" was a corps of "guardians." This would consist of a civilian auxiliary to the local police force and would include watchmen of all kinds, playground supervisors, custodians of children in public places, and persons who would perform other custodial, informational, and related functions. Another category was a corps of teaching aides, who appear especially needed in the lower grades of elementary school. Health aides would render supportive services in providing medical and allied care in and out of hospitals. They would also serve as resource persons in providing information on the availability of health services. The position of home aides calls for people to visit households of the old and disabled to help them. Another task of the home aides would be to assist in caring for children whose parents are temporarily absent.

Several new positions of the type recommended have been tried on a limited basis in several cities. In Poughkeepsie, New York, Model Cities Director Marie Tarver obtained Federal funds for several new positions to better serve the city's depressed area. These include the positions of health aide, teacher aide, community service aide, homemaker aide, and public housing security officer.

Evaluations of paraprofessional programs indicate that they generally have good results. Frank Riessman, one of the original designers of the "new careers" program, points to many contributions of paraprofessionals in improving services to urban communities. These include reaching hitherto unreached people, providing new kinds of services, improving the performance and attitudes of professionals, and introducing a new community ethos into agencies that have limited ties to the community.[19] A 1971 book by Alan Gartner entitled *Paraprofessionals and Their Performance* provides much support for Riessman's view. Gartner not only found that paraprofessionals provide needed services to the community, but he performed a cost–benefit analysis to show that the money expended for their training and salaries made good sense in strict economic terms. He found that the resulting reduction in various costs, including those for welfare and the criminal justice system, amounted to a twelvefold return.[20]

The use of paraprofessionals is still in its experimental stages and a few wrinkles have shown up in several programs. Educational consultant Carol Ginsburg, who has evaluated several programs involving the use of teaching aides in schools, has found many shortcomings. In New York City, for example, aides were misused by being assigned to meaningless duties by teachers to keep them out of the way. In other instances aides were encouraged to severely discipline the children to keep order by instilling fear. Ginsburg feels that these abuses can be corrected with "more adequate role definition and training of paraprofessionals." Of equal importance, according to Ginsburg, is training for the professionals who are to work with the aides.[21]

The use of paraprofessionals on a broad scale will require a major governmental financial commitment. In 1972 Senator Alan Cranston of California introduced a bill to provide ten billion dollars to create more than a million jobs in public service and in private companies under Federal contract. Many of the positions would be in existing job classifications, including policemen and firemen, while others would be paraprofessional positions intended to serve as a stepping-stone for the unskilled.

One obstacle that must be overcome in providing upgrading opportunities is inflexible and often irrelevant test requirements, such as rigid civil service tests. One critic of these tests, manpower specialist and community leader Lawrence Briggs, points out that many questions are not relevant to the duties of the job involved and some, such as vocabulary questions, seem to be written from a middle-class perspective. But rather than attempt the cumbersome process of getting the tests changed, Briggs advocates intensive counseling to enable poverty-area residents to pass.[22]

Rigid testing in private industry also represents an obstacle to upgrading for entry-level workers. Good jobs in the construction trade, for example, are largely controlled by trade unions that require tests. An organization, RTP, Inc. (Recruitment and Training Program), funded by Federal and foundation monies, helps low-skill persons pass the tests and meet other job requirements. According to RTP Executive Director Ernest Green, the organization has the two-fold purpose of locating people with the potential for upgrading and bringing out this potential through short-term tutoring "to be certain they get through the requirement hurdles."[23]

In 1972 a book appeared criticizing government involvement in upgrading programs with the contention that the main obstacle in employment advancement is the prevailing occupational structure. The author points out that there are many low-skill jobs that must be performed and only a limited number of higher-level positions to which people can advance. "An increase in the pool of eligibles not accompanied by an increase in the number of available positions," states the author, "may yield an increase in the number of disappointed and dissatisfied workers."[24] He therefore recommended that efforts should be made to alter the occupational structure of industry, such as through the further application of automation. But he also saw value in continuing upgrading training for workers, particularly blacks. He felt that this would at least put them on a par with workers eligible for advancement and would make them more competitive for the better jobs that now exist and will become available in the future.

One method within the realm of government jurisdiction is minimum wage legislation. Minimum wage legislation can be looked upon as a way of helping to bring about employment upgrading. As the minimum wage is raised, employers are forced to decide whether to eliminate their lowest–level jobs and let machines take over, or restructure the jobs so that they will involve a greater skill level to justify the higher wages mandated by law.

Urban Policies

Beyond focusing on opening up meaningful employment opportunities for the unskilled, the government should be concerned with its overall urban policies. The prevailing welfare system, for example, often discourages unskilled people from seeking employment. Amory Bradford, a student of the ghettos of California, commented: "You're going to have to do something about welfare to get a lot of people interested in training and jobs. For many, they are better off with welfare payments than they will be when they are taking training and sometimes when they finally get jobs."[25]

The problem is that the present welfare system permits individuals to receive welfare payments only when they are not working and have no source of income. Since welfare payments are determinted by family size, the head of a large family may not be able to get a job that provides an income equal to the payments from welfare. The welfare system should be changed to provide incentives to individuals who want to work.

The same shortcoming in the welfare system exists in many job training programs which insist that only individuals without jobs be allowed to participate. Programs with this requirement often bypass the working poor. Many training programs admit only heads of households; thus a wife who must obtain a job to help support the family is denied training. It has been found that this encourages male desertion and the creation of female–headed households. Lester Thurow, professor of economics at Harvard University, agrees with government manpower officials that first priority in training programs should be given to heads of households, but he suggests a basis that would make secondary wage earners also eligible. "To be eligible for the program," he recommends, "a married woman must have worked full time in the labor force for two years unless she comes from a family where the family income is below the poverty line."[26]

Beyond reevaluating welfare and job training policies, the government should look for ways to revitalize urban areas with the objective of stimulating economic growth and thereby creating new jobs. One suggestion is for the Federal government to sponsor a massive, nationwide public works program that would at once give cities needed new facilities, such as water pollution control works, while at the same time providing new employment opportunities in the lucrative construction trades. This suggestion came from city planner Roger Starr, who stated it as follows:

> To narrow the income gap between the poor and the middle class, the cities must provide vastly increased economic opportunities; for example, the construction of a total national waste treatment program which would, under direct Federal auspices, provide wholly new waste collection and disposal systems. Construction of such a system would not only represent an inescapable investment in the future health of the nation, but might, if developed with statesmanship, open direct employment opportunities in the construction fields for many young adults now only on the edges of the job market.[27]

In recommending this approach, Starr remarked, "In the absence of such an expansion, all the talk about training and

education as a cure for underemployment will merely determine which members of the total work force are to be the
ones left out in the cold."[28] He further noted that this program
would help not only present ghetto residents get a meaningful
job, but would also help newcomers to the cities. "The new
arrival must be prepared for fruitful work, not merely through
the development of his urban traits and specific skills, but
through the preparation of a healthy and bustling economy
that must be waiting for him."[29]

A Federally–funded job placement program in Bingham-
ton, New York, fell short of its goal to place a certain number
of poverty–area residents in jobs. Michael Murphy, director
of the Model Cities Agency that monitors the program, explained that the project's shortcoming was due largely to the
area's depressed economy. "How can you expect employers to
hire new people when they're laying off their present workers?"
asks Murphy. "Even when a company starts hiring again, their
first preference will be those they have laid off since they already have the training and experience."[30]

Critics of government manpower programs have long
pointed out that while there has been an emphasis on training for jobs, not enough has been done to make sure that jobs
are available. A recent assessment of manpower programs and
other government "anti–poverty strategy" over the last ten
years criticized the apparent assumption by government officials "that the cause of poverty lay in the disadvantaged condition of individuals, not in the failure of the job market."[31]

While striving to stimulate the economy of cities to help
ghetto inhabitants, government should seek out new resources
to provide increased public services in poverty areas. Nathan
Wright, in his analysis of problems facing the urban poor, has
attributed many ghetto problems to the dwindling resources
of cities due to the flight of whites and industry to the suburbs.
He notes, for example, "Approximately one–half of Newark's
200,000 jobs are filled by people who live in the suburbs."[32]
Yet this city, he is surprised to learn, has no commuter taxes

or any other mechanisms to obtain economic contributions from those who benefit from the city but provide nothing to help. Wright contends that a substantial amount of police protection is needed in cities during the day because of the high daytime (commuter) population, with the result that cities cannot afford adequate police protection at night.

Measures must also be taken to allow the city's poor to take advantage of the jobs that are becoming increasingly available in suburban areas. A team of urban planners reported, "The suburbanization of population and jobs in the metropolitan regions is an accomplished fact." They recommended, "Rather than fighting this movement, urban development policy should work with it to assure equal access to suburban land and jobs for all citizens of the region."[33] For this, they recommend that low–rent, multifamily housing be constructed in the suburbs and cheaper, more efficient mass transit be provided to suburban job centers.

Since the working poor are concentrated in cities, the elected officials there must bear major responsibility for initiating ideas and programs to deal with the problem. Mount Vernon, New York, despite its relative small size (population: 72,778), has introduced many successful programs that have placed ghetto residents into meaningful jobs. The driving force behind many of these efforts has been Mayor August P. Petrillo.

Mayor Petrillo's success appears to derive from his background as a former industrialist and business leader in the community. He knows the realities of the business world and the motives of businessmen upon whom employment programs must depend. He knows that altruism among businessmen usually stops after an annual donation to a favorite charity is made. Few businessmen will rearrange their business to accommodate an employment program, at least not unless the program can be shown to clearly benefit their operation by reducing costs and/or increasing output. The mayor also knows that businessmen are not averse to misusing employment programs if it means making a buck. "I've known of situations in which companies would fire workers only to re-hire them with government subsidy monies," states the mayor. Mayor Petrillo's programs have emphasized training before placement in jobs. As he says, "The undereducated, under-skilled minority worker has enough strikes against him without being thrown into a job without adequate preparation."[34]

The elected officials of cities must be prepared to work closely with poverty–area leaders and constantly maintain communication and credibility. They must also resist the temp-tation to manipulate programs in these areas for political pur-poses. It is to the credit of Syracuse Mayor Lee Alexander, a Democrat, that he decided to keep Model Cities Director Regi-nald Gary, an experienced and enterprising professional, de-spite the fact that Gary had been appointed by the mayor's Republican predecessor.

Policies and actions of government should emphasize long–term, permanent solutions to problems, rather than take the quickest steps available to temporarily alleviate or "cover–up" the situation. The traditional government approach to problem–solving was noted by one observer at the time of the Newark riot of 1968 when he said, "The main emphasis of a government remedial program seems likely to be on ending the riots rather than dealing with the racial and economic problem."[35]

Perhaps the "crisis management" that typifies so many government actions explains not only the failure of many pro-grams but the fact that sometimes they seem to work at cross–purposes. In a section of the 1972 *Manpower Report of the President* entitled "Lessons Learned," duplications and con-flicts between government programs were cited. For example, as the Department of Labor was eliminating programs that aided teacher training when a decline in the demand for teachers was imminent, the National Defense Education Act gave support for teacher education. The report recommended that the government should better coordinate its programs and policies.[36]

There is substantial evidence that when a crisis develops and the government is forced to deal with the problems of the ghetto, the typical approach is to cut planning short and do something quickly to pacify residents and appease community leaders. A comparison between the approach of the government in dealing with the Vietnamese and the ghetto population was drawn by Tom Hayden. "Compare the pacification plans prepared for Vietnamese peasants by the Central Intelligence Agency (CIA)," suggests Hayden, "with the analysis of Watts made by the national commission headed by—why not? —the former head of the CIA." He notes, "one blames the Viet Cong terrorists—the other blames the 'hotheads' in the Negro community. Both justify the acts of the army. Both suggest more counseling service and economic aid administered by leaders loyal and responsible to the government. And both leave the 'natives' nothing but anger."[37]

The government's approach in dealing with urban problems has also been condemned for its traditional emphasis on improving physical appearance rather than social conditions. Nathan Wright criticizes the shortsightedness of this approach. He recommends that the priority of the government should be on "human rehabilitation rather than on clearing up physical blight."[38]

There is a fear among some observers that the General Revenue Sharing Act of 1972 will encourage cities to emphasize physical improvement rather than the social programs. The wording of the legislation indeed seems to favor expenditures for physical projects. Moreover, there is no provision for meaningful citizen participation and only limited accountability on the part of local officials. Early indications reveal that the only two nonphysical areas in which large sums of money will be spent are for law enforcement and education. But even in the area of education, to spend money without making necessary reforms is, according to Robert McAlpine of the National League of Cities, "to make a bad system worse."[39]

13

A ROLE FOR INDUSTRY

Since the beginning of the United States, government has struggled with strategies and programs to alleviate social problems. Some of the efforts have indeed been misguided or have lacked real commitment, but American industry has remained generally aloof. Only recently and by no means universally has industry begun to recognize that it too must play a role in helping to ameliorate social problems.

Several factors underlie industry's traditional disregard for social problems. The free enterprise system, with its emphasis on individualism, promotes the attitude that each person should be responsible for solving his own problems. Moreover, the primary function of a business enterprise being to maximize profit, those in charge have viewed nonprofit-making activities as inappropriate and wasteful. Even philanthropy by businessmen has often been engaged in for self-serving ends.

Today there are still many conservative businessmen who shrug off any social conscience and merely assume the traditional nonparticipative role. But there are also many who have become greatly concerned and now accept a substantial amount of social responsibility in their business lives. Industry must assist in dealing with the problem of the working poor if real progress is to be made; the fact that 80 percent of the workers in the United States are found in private industry bears this out. [1]

Industry's Stake

Industry's traditional disregard for the social implications of its actions has come under sharp criticism in recent years. Nathan Wright has outspokenly stated, "It should have been made clear to every organization in the land, which has the privilege of serving the public for private profit, that to conduct one's business in such a manner as to create or aggravate social problems, is a crime against society."[2]

Many critics have pointed to industry's specific social responsibility to treat their workers as human beings, to recognize their human needs, and to take a greater concern in helping them grow in their work. "It is in this area," writes one concerned observer, "that private industry must make its greatest contribution to social justice."[3]

Besides the moral obligation, solution of the problem has clear dollar–and–cents implications for business. In a report prepared for businessmen by the Research Institute of America, industry was encouraged to make more of a financial investment in attempting to provide better job opportunities for residents of poverty areas. The report explained, as follows, that this investment could lead to long–term economic benefits:

> In the final analysis, the prime prerequisite must be a willingness to take a longer-range view of costs. No one—not even the most deeply committed—can pretend that the immediate, short-term costs to business will be small. But when the investment is measured against the long-range benefits to the company, the community, and the economy in general, another kind of balance sheet emerges. Call it "investment in the future," call it "insurance," or call it "preventive measures," each company will have to decide for itself how much red ink it can live with in the meantime.[4]

This report was issued toward the end of the 1960's shortly after the urban riots that caused so much damage to businesses located in inner cities. The report's reference to "preventive measures" took into account these disorders. In addition to the physical damage done to business establishments, operations may be adversely affected by in–plant personnel problems involving racial tension and employee morale.

Cleveland official David Hill, in encouraging businessmen to give their full cooperation to government–sponsored employment programs, told them that their involvement would help them maintain good relations with the black community and be a business advantage. He encouraged businessmen to ask themselves the following questions in making a decision on whether or not to become involved: "What do we have invested in this city? How can we keep our insurance rates down?"[5]

Black consultant Leonard Fonville, who worked for the U.S. Department of Labor in the late 1960's, found that a large white–owned department store on the fringe of a black ghetto was unusually receptive to a job upgrading program he had designed for entry–level black workers. "This store was apparently high on the list of places to be burned," states Fonville in explaining the reason for this receptivity.[6]

Industry actually has much more at stake than the possibility of loss due to racial upheavals. Underemployment of workers usually represents underutilization of manpower. Many workers trapped in unskilled jobs have the potential and aptitude to become highly productive skilled technicians or perceptive members of the supervisory–management team. By not providing a means for them to escape their situation and rise to their true level, a wasteful practice is followed, as wasteful as discarding by–products in a refinery before their potential use is explored.

Suggested Steps

If industry becomes convinced that doing something about the problem of limited employment opportunities for blacks is important for itself as well as for society, the question may well be asked, "What can be done about it?" After all, do not menial, unskilled jobs exist out of necessity? Doesn't somebody have to do them? The answer, of course, is yes! But even so, business can take actions that would help alleviate the most a'arming aspects of this situation.

The first step that businessmen should take is to view their workers as human beings with human needs. Avenues might be explored to make unskilled jobs more bearable. One study found that the very knowledge among workers that efforts are being made by their company to improve conditions and make their work more tolerable serves in itself to increase job satisfaction.[7]

Company efforts to assist unskilled workers requires sensitivity to the special circumstances of blacks in America, but instead of such sensitivity, the old stereotypes have largely prevailed. The Riot Commission took note of the fact that few businessmen seem to understand their black workers:

> Typically, we locate the problem in the Negro himself. We say, for example, that Negroes are lazy, irresponsible, and don't want to work. Then we offer them the most menial, the dullest, the poorest paid job in our society and, sure enough, there are some of them who don't want to work.[8]

Businessmen who make little effort to understand the attitudes and behavior of their black employees often say that the cultural differences between their workers and themselves present an insurmountable obstacle to communication and understanding. This attitude came out in a sensitivity session observed by this writer when a white manager commented to a black worker, "We don't have the same experience or the same level of knowledge that you have." But the black worker was unconvinced; "You don't have to be a sociologist, you just have to be alive," he said.

It is necessary for employers to treat their unskilled workers with dignity and respect—not necessarily because their
jobs warrant such treatment, but rather because as human
beings the workers are entitled to it. Companies, therefore,
should strive to improve working conditions. One improvement
would be formal orientation sessions for all new employees
regardless of job level to cover such items as company background and operations, future plans, advancement opportunities, grievance procedures, and the role of the workers' jobs in
the total operation. Such knowledge on the part of entry–level
workers makes them more content and enhances their self–
respect because they see their job as more significant than they
would have otherwise viewed it.

Another approach that should be taken where possible is
to provide new job titles and higher wages for entry–level jobs
to give them some degree of prestige. In commenting on this
approach, an industrial psychologist observed: "The woman
who works in a carry–out shop as a waitress is doing essentially
the same thing as the airline stewardess."[9] After noting that
low–skill positions will, probably continue to exist in large
numbers for some time in the future, he recommended, "Let's
upgrade the job, instead of upgrading the person."

In addition to upgrading the image of entry–level positions, something should be done about the work tasks. A recent study found that a few minor modifications in jobs involving repetitive tasks can make them less boring. A change of
pace can be accomplished by rearranging job tasks. The work
could be made more interesting by giving more tasks to perform; instead of the job involving one manual operation, it
might be restructured to consist of two or three.

These are not very dramatic suggestions. The fact is,
however, that even mild job improvements such as these have
been rare in industry This has prompted one critic to say:
"The trouble with industrial employment is that it never attempts to discover what it hires when it hires a man."[10]

Perhaps as important as changing the attitude of un-

skilled workers is the need to do something about their supervisor's attitudes. Entry–level workers are commonly treated
with scorn and contempt by foremen and supervisors, perhaps
because of the insecurity and discontent that sometimes exists
in these people who are often only one step removed from
those whom they oversee. As long as management does nothing
to discourage such treatment, any efforts to help workers
adjust to their jobs will be futile.

Often, white supervisors' treatment of black workers
clearly reflects prejudicial feelings. The same may be true of
the way black workers are treated by whites on the occupational level. Where prejudice and racial polarization are apparent, management should quickly respond. Since white
workers are often prejudiced because they feel that blacks pose
a competitive threat, management should make clear that
their fears are unwarranted. Industrial studies have provided
evidence that there are no "economic benefits for white workers
to be derived from discrimination against minority workers."[11]

Another concern of managers should be to establish lines
of communication between themselves and all of their employees. This will help in formulating personnel policies by
providing information about the problems and perceptions of
workers. The workers, meanwhile, could be kept informed
about company plans and policies, giving them a greater sense
of personal worth and strengthening their identity with the
organization. Bulletin boards, newsletters, and suggestion
boxes are methods that have been used successfully to improve
in–plant communications. An article in an industrial trade
journal pointed out that in the absence of a good communication system, management often does not learn about problems
among workers until they have reached the critical point;
racial tension is one example. A "good feedback information
system" could enable management to detect early signs of
such problems and take remedial action before it is too late.[12]

Another area of recommended action for industry is to
develop ways to reduce the dead–end aspect of most entry–

level jobs. One method would be to restructure jobs to create a network of positions varying in complexity and responsibility. Such "job ladders," with step increases in pay and responsibility open to entry–level workers, have been established by only a few companies. A survey conducted by the Urban Coalition in 1969 revealed that, "While many companies are examining upgrading and job restructuring possibilities, only a very few upgrading efforts are now taking place.[13] In many instances government assistance to companies in job restructuring is provided by occupation research analysts on the staffs of state employment service agencies.

Regardless of whether or not career ladders exist in a company, every effort should be made to fill skilled and supervisory positions from within. The time and energy devoted to recruiting outside for these jobs could often be better applied to developing in–plant programs that would give unskilled workers the technical and supervisory skills needed to fill the vacancies. When entry–level workers observe upgrading taking place in their ranks, their morale improves noticeably. A report prepared by Skill Upgrading, Inc., in Baltimore, revealed that unskilled workers could be trained for supervisory positions in as short a period as five weeks.[14]

A supervisor who comes from the ranks of workers whom he now must supervise sometimes experiences problems, especially if he is black and his workers are mostly white. But problems can be avoided if the new supervisor is given proper training and the workers are made to see that management is fully behind him. If the workers are mostly black, it is a different story entirely. As one manpower expert has observed, "Black supervisors generally relate better to hardcore trainees, know more about their background, and can provide stronger supervision."[15]

An article in the *Wall Street Journal* entitled "Hiring Is Just the Beginning" was aimed at businessmen and criticized them for their typical feelings that simply placing unskilled blacks in any jobs in their company is enough to satisfy their social obligation. It was pointed out that helping workers obtain promotions is often more important to them than getting a job in the first place. The article went on to say that the criteria governing promotions in industry are often unrealistic and make it especially difficult for minority workers to advance. It cited a survey which found that much of what managers look for in people in considering them for higher–level jobs seems to be based more on "middle–class values and attitudes" rather than on talents that are genuinely needed to perform the job.[16]

Some companies have recently begun to reevaluate the interviewing and testing practices used in the placement and promotion of workers. They have found many to be "culturally biased" and to present unnecessary obstacles for minority workers. Indeed, questions on many job tests bear no relation to work functions or skill requirements or may be clearly middle–class oriented.

It goes without saying that employers should avoid all conscious discriminatory practices and immediately discard any that may be in existence. Besides damaging the morale and consequently the performance of black workers, discriminatory practices are costly because full advantage is not being taken of the total available manpower pool. Accordingly, a study found that in the more competitive industries—those most concerned with costs—discriminatory practices are less frequent.[17]

It was disclosed earlier in discussing the attitudes and perceptions of black workers that discriminatory practices, and even the intimation of such practices, intensify work dissatisfaction. Companies should make every attempt to integrate higher job levels racially so that even the appearance of prejudice will be removed. Several companies that established plants in ghetto areas and recruited the residents in an attempt to convince the local black community of their equal opportunity employment policies, were nevertheless viewed with suspicion and mistrust. Although much of their work force was black, they failed to bring blacks into supervisory and management positions. "A new plant in a ghetto is fine," commented Berkely Burrell, president of the National Business League, "so long as the ghetto residents manage most of it and exercise some degree of meaningful control over its future."[18]

Slant–Finn Incorporated, a manufacturing firm in New York visited by this writer, has made serious efforts to upgrade its black workers to skilled and supervisory positions and has even placed an upgraded black worker in the position of plant personnel manager. The company has found that the morale of black workers greatly improved as a result of these efforts.

It was noted in an earlier chapter that there is a high degree of interrelatedness between a person's experience in the work setting and his after–work activities. In striving to improve the situation of the working poor, employers should not confine their efforts to the work setting. They should consider, for example, organizing outside activities for workers that involve their families and sponsoring self–help projects in the communities. The Westinghouse Corporation, a large employer of blacks in Baltimore, has financed a multiservice center located in the heart of Baltimore's black ghetto. Professionals on the Westinghouse payroll comprise the staff of the center, while a board of directors made up of local residents establishes its policies and monitors its operation.

Employers have found that involvement in their workers' communities enhance attachment of employees to the company. Another motive for striving to improve the after–hours lives of a company's workers is that unsatisfactory job performance is often directly related to conditions in the home and the community. Absenteeism and lateness among workers, for example, is often due to circumstances over which they have little control. A study conducted for businessmen by the Research Institute of America pointed out that, "Poor transportation facilities are the primary cause of absenteeism and tardiness among workers from the inner city poverty neighborhoods."[19] A few companies have helped establish day care centers for black women who would have had to depend on costly and unreliable baby sitters in order to work. These women now have the opportunity to become steady workers.

Employers should also take an interest in unskilled blacks presently without jobs. The National Alliance of Businessmen, formed to attack the problem of "the hard–core unemployed," has found that providing just any job for unskilled blacks is not enough. It has therefore concentrated its efforts on "finding productive jobs, not simply make–work or 'dead end' positions."[20] The businessmen's group has found that to place the unskilled in good jobs requires "relevant training programs."

Corporations making an effort to provide good training and decent jobs to the unskilled have found that men "are now being unlocked from lives of frustration and despair and are being given new hope."[21] Many companies are apparently content simply to place unskilled blacks in any jobs. Noting this, it has been stated: "Much of today's recruiting leaves a hard–core Negro about where he started: A little better than nowhere."[22] One black worker trapped in an entry–level job reflected on the failure of industry to live up to the promise of good jobs: "A Nigger is still a Nigger."[23]

Some employers believe that creating nonpurposeful jobs for unskilled blacks is worthwhile. The fact is that make–work positions are quickly recognized as such both by those hired for them and by the other workers. The newly hired workers are uncomfortable and dissatisfied in their roles and experience the rejection and resentment of the other workers. One report notes:

> A basic consideration is whether the rank-and-file worker, first-line supervisor, and personnel staff see the incoming hard-core hirees as necessary or superfluous. Fellow workers and supervisors tend not to resent having to help a disadvantaged individual even if they think he is a bit slow, if he is needed to get the work out.[24]

Many companies run into problems with unions in undertaking special hiring or training programs. This may be the fault of the employers, who often fail to notify the union. Aspects of a hiring or training program touch upon union contract items and legitimately concerned the members. Many employers have found that the best tactic is to bring union officials in on their plans at the earliest possible stage. Besides avoiding later resistance, union suggestions may help make the programs more workable.

Organized labor has indeed shown some commitment to the development of minority manpower. In 1968 the AFL–CIO established the Human Resources Development Institute (HRDI) to assist industry in obtaining Federal aid for the recruiting, hiring, and training of the hard–core unemployed. The more than 130 HRDI staff representatives in the country also work closely with local unions and management in ironing out any differences that may arise during the operational period of the contract. According to HRDI national director Julius F. Rothman, uppermost in the objectives of the program is to provide "good jobs at decent pay."[25]

Another aspect of the HRDI project is the "Buddy Program" which was developed to assist with the problem of retaining newly hired hard–core recruits. According to John T. Burnell, HRDI northeastern regional director, the buddy, a trained union member, provides the personal support on–the–job that many disadvantaged need, especially in the early days.[26]

Perhaps more effective approaches to the problem of confinement of blacks to menial jobs are possible. As black leader Bayard Rustin has pointed out, "The business community in the United States has proven by our GNP that it is the most imaginative, creative group of men on earth when it comes to knowing how to make money. . . ." In a statement made before the Equal Employment Opportunity Commission, Rustin said: "The issue is not that American business is so unintelligent that it does not know how to solve the problem. They have on the drawing board the kinds of automobiles we will have in 1980. They know what the GNP will be, according to the way in which they are going to act, in the next twenty–five years. . . . The problem is the problem of will."[27]

The future direction is clear. Government and industry must jointly strive to create the conditions under which un-skilled workers have a chance to learn higher–skilled, eco-nomically more rewarding work and to provide desirable job opportunities for them. This will result in increasing the level of responsibility and personal adjustment of these workers, who will then be in a better position to control their own destinies and contribute to the welfare of society.

NOTES AND REFERENCES

Chapter 1

1. Brennan, *The Making of a Moron*, p. 151. (In the notes references are in abbreviated form. Full citations are given in the Bibliography.)
2. *Report of the National Advisory Commission on Civil Disorders,* p. 132.
3. Ibid., p. 140.
4. Wilensky, "Work, Careers, and Social Integration," p. 544.
5. U.S. Department of Labor, *Manpower Report* (April, 1972), p. 22.
6. Spring, et al., p. 51.
7. U.S. Department of Labor, *Manpower Report* (March, 1972), pp. 38-39.
8. Newcomb and Simmons, "Keep Employees Informed," p. 69.

Chapter 2

1. Wright, *Ready to Riot,* p. 80.
2. Ibid., p. 8.

Chapter 3

1. Simon, *The Shape of Automation,* p. 50.
2. Anderson, *Dimensions of Work,* p. 146.
3. Anderson and Ishwaran, *Urban Sociology,* p. 148.
.4. Morse and Weiss, "The Function and Meaning of Work and the Job," p. 192.
5. Brayfield and Wells, "Interrelationships Among Measures of Job Satisfaction and General Satisfaction," p. 204.
6. Weiss and Riesman, "Some Issues in the Future of Leisure," in Smigel, *Work and Leisure,* p. 169.
7. Blum, *Toward a Democratic Work Process,* p. 98.
8. Ferdynand Zweig, *The Worker in an Affluent Society,* p. 197.
9. Ibid., pp. 197-198.
10. Schneider, *Industrial Sociology,* p. 353.
11. Anderson, *Dimensions of Work,* p. 9.
12. Lefkowitz, "Self-Esteem of Industrial Workers," pp. 521-28.
13. Zweig, op. cit., p. 85.
14. Aiken et al., *Economic Failure, Alienation, and Extremism,* 1968.
15. Guy Hunter (ed.), *Industrialization and Race Relations,* p. 250.
16. Schneider, op. cit., p. 379.
17. Hawley, *Human Economy,* p. 228.
18. Levine, *Workers Vote,* pp. 300-17.
19. Aiken, et al., op. cit., p. 127.
20. Form and Miller, *Industry, Labor, and Community,* p. 415.
21. Sobin, *Dynamics of Community Change,* 1968, p. 84.

Chapter 4

1. Brennan, op. cit., p. 14.
2. Marx, *Wage-Labour and Capital,* pp. 44-45.
3. Lipsitz, "Work Life and Political Attitudes," pp. 951-62.
4. Turnbull, *The Changing Faces of Economic Security,* p. 132.
5. Marx, op. cit., p. 45.
6. U.S. National Advisory Commission and Civil Disorders, Hearings, p. 61.
7. Spring, et al., op. cit., p. 42.
8. Chinoy, *Automobile Workers and the American Dream,* p. 15.
9. U.S. National Advisory Commission on Civil Disorders, Hearings, p. 31.

10. U.S. Department of Labor, Bureau of Labor Statistics, *The Negroes in the United States,* p. 162.

11. U.S. Department of Labor, Bureau of Labor Statistics and U.S. Department of Commerce, Bureau of the Census, *Social and Economic Conditions of Negroes in the United States,* p. 41.

12. Semple, "New U.S. Report Finds Few Negroes in White Collar Jobs," p. 45.

13. Ibid., p. 45.

14. U.S. Equal Employment Opportunity Commission, *Hearings on Discrimination in White Collar Employment,* p. 531.

15. Baltimore Community Relations Commission, *Report of Employment Breakdown by Race,* p. 4.

16. Greater Cleveland Plans for Progress Council, *1967 Negro Employment Breakthrough Survey,* p. 2.

17. U.S. Department of Labor, Bureau of Labor Statistics, *The Negroes in the United States,* p. 111.

18. Glazer and Moynihan, *Beyond the Melting Pot,* p. 30.

19. U.S. Department of Labor, Bureau of Labor Statistics, *The Negroes in the United States,* p. 128.

20. U.S. National Advisory Commission on Civil Disorders, Hearings, p. 56.

21. U.S. Department of Labor, *Manpower Report of the President,* p. 46.

22. Habbe, *Company Experience with Negro Employment,* p. 47.

23. U.S. Equal Employment Opportunity Commission, op. cit., p. 316.

24. Weaver, *Negro Labor: A National Problem,* p. 97.

25. U.S. National Advisory Commission on Civil Disorders, Hearings, p. 62.

26. Cassell, "Business and the Community," p. 373.

27. Mayfield, "Equal Opportunity at the Third and Toughest Stage," p. 8.

28. Habbe, op. cit., p. 46.

29. Leggett, *Class, Race, and Labor,* p. 11.

30. Silberman, *Crisis in Black and White,* p. 243.

Chapter 5

1. Baldwin, *The Fire Next Time,* p. 114.

2. Woodson, *African Heroes and Heroines,* 1944.

3. Baldwin, op. cit., p. 114-15.

4. Dynes et al., *Social Problems,* 1964.

5. "A Mother Can't Do a Man's Job," *Newsweek*, p. 41-42.
6. Grier and Cobbs, *Black Rage*, 1968.
7. Lefcourt, "Risk Taking in Negro and White Adults," pp. 765-70.
8. Miller, "Some Thoughts on Reform," in Shostak and Gomberg, *Blue-Collar World*, p. 305.
9. Baldwin, op. cit., p. 139.
10. "The Urban Crisis," p. 122.
11. Heacock, *Understanding the Negro Protest*, p. 39.
12. Becker, *The Economics of Discrimination*, p. 124.
13. Ibid., p. 73.
14. Ibid., p. 123.
15. Habbe, op. cit., p. 21.
16. U.S. Department of Labor, Bureau of Labor Statistics and U.S. Department of Commerce, Bureau of the Census, *Social and Economic Conditions of Negroes in the United States*, p. XI.
17. Gregory, *Nigger*, pp. 78-79.
18. Pettigrew, *A Profile of the Negro-American*, p. 191.
19. Ibid., p. 191.
20. Waterman, "Local Issues in the Urban War on Poverty," p. 58.
21. Sobin, "Why Increase Citizen Participation Among Ghetto Residents," pp. 368-9.
22. Kafoglis, "The Economics of the Community Action Program," p. 74.
23. Brown, "The Fomented Conflict," p. 180.
24. Shostak, "Promoting Participation of the Poor," p. 67.
25. Zweig, op. cit., p. 55.
26. Miller, "Some Thoughts on Reform," in Shostak and Gomberg, op. cit., p. 303.
27. Zweig, op. cit., p. 85.
28. Caplow, *The Sociology of Work*, p. 77.
29. Schneider, *Industrial Sociology*, p. 405.
30. Becker, op. cit., p. 125.
31. Wright, *Black Power and Urban Unrest*, p. 50.
32. "Blow-Up in the Cities," p. 3.
33. Hayden, *A View of the Poverty Program*, p. 5.
34. Silberman, *Crisis in Black and White*, p. 35.
35. Heacock, op. cit., p. 12.

Chapter 6

1. Morse and Weiss, op. cit., p. 198.
2. Price and Levinson, "Work and Mental Illness," in Shostak and Gomberg, op. cit., p. 398.
3. Cleeton, *Making Work Human*, p. 37.
4. Arthur Kornhauser, "Toward An Assessment of the Mental Health of Factory Workers," pp. 43-46.
5. Mumford, *The Condition of Man*, p. 175.
6. Riessman (ed.), *Up From Poverty*, p. 27.
7. Brennan, op. cit., p. 40.
8. Zweig, op. cit., p. 55.
9. Pearlin, "Alienation From Work: A Study of Nursing Personnel," p. 315.
10. Anderson, *Dimensions of Work*, p. 86.
11. Tausky and Wilson, "Work Attachment Among Black Men," p. 6.
12. Champagne and King, "Job Satisfaction Factors Among Under-privileged Workers," p. 429.
13. Wills, *The Second Civil War*, p. 156.
14. U.S. National Advisory Commission on Civil Disorders, Hearings, p. 11.
15. Tausky and Wilson, op. cit., p. 9.
16. Ibid., p. 8.
17. U.S. Department of Labor, *Manpower Report* (April, 1968), p. 88.
18. Gregory, *The Shadow That Scares Me*, p. 159.
19. Leggett, op. cit., p. 98.
20. U.S. National Advisory Commission on Civil Disorders, Hearings, p. 158.
21. Rutledge and Gass, *Nineteen Negro Men: Personality and Manpower Retraining*, p. 16.

Chapter 7

1. Aiken et al., op. cit., p. 153.
2. Chinoy, op. cit.
3. Wilensky, "Work, Careers, and Social Integration," p. 301.
4. Greer, *The Emerging City, Myth and Reality*, p. 34.
5. Arnold Rose, *Sociology*, p. 330.
6. Form and Miller, op. cit., p. 645.

7. Smigel, op. cit., pp. 169-70.
8. Weiss and Riesman, "Some Issues in the Future of Leisure," in Smigel, *Work and Leisure*, p. 174.
9. Miller and Riessman, "The Working-Class Sub-Culture: A New View," in Shostak, op. cit., p. 33.
10. Hentoff, *The New Equality*, p. 100.
11. Aiken, et al., op. cit., p. 154.
12. Will and Vatter, op. cit., p. 28.

Chapter 8

1. Aiken et al., op. cit., p. 154.
2. Kornhouser et al., *When Labor Votes*, p. 194.
3. Hunter, *The Slums: Challenge and Response*, p. 225.
4. Anderson and Ishwaran, *Urban Sociology*, p. 147.
5. Miller, "The Political Potential of Class and Race," pp. 212-18.
6. Ibid.
7. Leggett, op. cit., p. 124.
8. Lipsitz, "Work Life and Political Attitudes," pp. 951-62.
9. Drucker, "Worker and Work in the Metropolis," p. 1,258.
10. Kornhouser et al., op. cit., p. 105.

Chapter 9

1. Lyndon B. Johnson, "Special Message to Congress," 1966.
2. Wright, *Ready to Riot,* p. 39.
3. Lincoln, *Sounds of Struggle*, p. 194.
4. Ibid., p. 194.
5. Starr, *The Living End: The City and Its Critics*, p. 99.
6. U.S. Department of Labor, Bureau of Labor Statistics, and U.S. Department of Commerce, Bureau of the Census, *Social and Economic Conditions of Negroes in the United States*, p. 65.
7. Wright, *Black Power and Urban Unrest*, p. 93.
8. Wright, *Ready to Riot,* p. 16.
9. Condon, *Cleveland: The Best Kept Secret*, p. 355.
10. Wright, *Ready to Riot*, p. 42.
11. Gregory, *The Shadow That Scares Me*, p. 112.
12. U.S. Department of Labor, *Manpower Report of the President,* March, 1972, p. 39.

13. Wetzel and Holland, "Poverty Areas of Our Major Cities," pp. 1,105-10.
14. Schnapper, "Notes and Comments—Consumer Legislation and the Poor," *Yale Law Journal*, p. 745.
15. Planning and Research Associates, *Economic Development Study: Mount Vernon Model Neighborhood, 1972*, pp. 37-38.
16. Harris, "Big Business Do-Gooders," p. 15.
17. U.S. Department of Labor, Bureau of Labor Statistics, and U.S. Department of Commerce, Bureau of the Census, *Social and Economic Conditions of Negroes in the United States*, p. XI.
18. Task Force on Economic Growth and Opportunity, *The Disadvantaged Poor: Education and Employment*, p. 229.
19. Duhl and Chayes, "Developing Human Resources," p. 404.
20. Berkely, "People: The New Voice In Renewal," p. 76.
21. Jeffers, *Living Poor*.
22. Wright, *Ready to Riot*, p. 17.
23. Bullough, "Alienation in the Ghetto," p. 469-78.
24. Wright, *Ready to Riot*, p. 117.
25. Waterman, "Local Issues in the Urban War on Poverty," p. 60.
26. Hayden, *Rebellion in Newark*, p. 6.
27. Levine, "Citizen Participation," p. 200.
28. Garrity, "Red Ink for Ghetto Industries," p. 4.
29. Herbers, "Economics Development of Blighted Inner-City Areas Is Running Into Snags," p. 72.
30. Ibid.

Chapter 10

1. Isenberg, *The City in Crisis*, p. 11.
2. U.S. Department of the Army, *Civil Disturbances and Disasters*, p. 3.
3. Heacock, op. cit., p. 6.
4. Ibid., p. 7.
5. Wright, *Ready to Riot*, p. 137.
6. Lincoln, *Sounds of the Struggle: Persons and Perspectives in Civil Rights*, p. 14.
7. Heacock, op. cit., p. 9.
8. "The Hard-Core Ghetto Mood," p. 31.
9. Ibid., p. 9.
10. Gregory, *The Shadow that Scares Me*, pp. 164-65.

11. Coles, "Like It Is in the Alley," p. 1,325.
12. Gregory, *The Shadow that Scares Me,* p. 148.
13. Ibid., p. 143.
14. Ibid., p. 144.
15. Cunningham, op. cit., p. 314.
16. Wright, *Ready to Riot,* pp. 2-3.
17. Ibid., p. 1.
18. Ibid., p. 6.
19. Hayden, *Rebellion in Newark,* p. 68.
20. Cunningham, op. cit., p. 64.
21. American Friends Service Committee, *Report on Baltimore Civil Disorders,* p. 5.
22. Arthur I. Waskow, *From Race Riot to Sit-In,* pp. 306-07.
23. U.S. National Advisory Commission on Civil Disorders, Hearings, p. 8.
24. Ibid., p. 162.
25. Toch, *The Social Psychology of Social Movements,* p. 10.
26. U.S. Department of Justice, *Detection of Potential Community Violence,* 1968.
27. Endleman, *Violence in the Streets,* 1968.
28. Borow, *Man in a World at Work,* p. XIV.
29. Ibid., p. XV.
30. Arthur Miller, "The Bored and the Violent," in Endleman, op. cit., p. 275.
31. U.S. National Advisory Commission on Civil Disorders, Hearings, p. 55.
32. John Paul Scott, "The Anatomy of Violence," in Endleman, op. cit., p. 70.
33. Zweig, op. cit., pp. 202-04.
34. Clark, "The Wonder Is There Have Been So Few Riots," in Endleman, op. cit., p. 287.
35. Report of the National Advisory Commission on Civil Disorders, p. 11.
36. Leggett, op. cit., p. 4.
37. Wright, *Ready to Riot,* p. 140.
38. Hunter, Guy, op. cit., p. 235.
39. Gartner, *Problem Identified, Solution Awry,* p. 7.
40. Weaver, op. cit., p. IX.
41. Brennan, op. cit., p. 165.
42. Ibid., p. 33.
43. Gregory, *The Shadow that Scares Me,* p. 88.

44. Clark, "The Wonder Is There Have Been So Few Riots," in Endleman, op. cit., p. 288.
45. Toch, *The Social Psychology of Social Movements,* p. 12.
46. Silberman, *Crisis in Black and White,* p. 357.
47. Bradford, *Oakland's Not for Burning,* p. 206.
48. Leggett, op. cit., p. 152.
49. U.S. National Advisory Commission on Civil Disorders, Hearings, p. 197.
50. "Upgraded Workers," p. 1.

Chapter 11

1. U.S. National Advisory Commission on Civil Disorders, Hearings, p. 182.
2. U.S. Department of Labor, *Manpower Report of the President,* April, 1968, p. 34.
3. U.S. Department of Labor, *Manpower Report of the President,* January, 1969, p. 44.
4. Wright, *Ready to Riot,* p. 68.
5. Ibid., p. 71.
6. Toch, *The Social Psychology of Social Movements,* p. 118.
7. U.S. National Advisory Commission on Civil Disorders, Hearings, p. 14.
8. Herbers, op. cit., p. 1.
9. Ibid., p. 71.
10. U.S. Equal Employment Opportunity Commission, *Hearings on Discrimination in White Collar Employment,* pp. 516-17.
11. U.S. National Advisory Commission on Civil Disorders, Hearings, p. 59.
12. Max Lerner, "The Negro American and His City," pp. 1,403-04.
13. U.S. National Advisory Commission on Civil Disorders, Hearings, p. 122.
14. Champagne and King, op. cit., p. 429.
15. Personal interview.

Chapter 12

1. Grier and Cobbs, op. cit., p. 212.
2. Wright, *Ready to Riot,* p. 83.

3. Ibid., p. 93.
4. Ibid., p. 109.
5. Hayden, *A View of the Poverty Program*, p. 15.
6. Hentoff, op. cit., p. 179.
7. U.S. National Advisory Commission on Civil Disorders, Hearings, p. 185.
8. Bradford, op. cit., p. 207.
9. U.S. National Advisory Commission on Civil Disorders, Hearings, p. 11.
10. U.S. Equal Employment Opportunity Commission, *Hearings on Discrimination in White Collar Employment*, p. 504.
11. Ibid., p. 493.
12. Herbers, "Gains Are Made in Federal Drive for Negro Hiring," p. 71.
13. Banfield, "Why Government Cannot Solve the Urban Problems," p. 1,232.
14. Personal interview.
15. Personal interview.
16. Reissman, *Up From Poverty*.
17. Silberman, *Crisis in Black and White*, p. 246.
18. Rohrlich, "Work and Income Policies for the Negro in Urban Slums," pp. 78-93.
19. Gartner, *Paraprofessionals and Their Performance*, p. vii.
20. Ibid., p. 107.
21. Personal interview.
22. Personal interview.
23. Personal interview.
24. Brecher, *Upgrading Blue Collar and Service Workers*, p. 105.
25. Bradford, op. cit., p. 76.
26. U.S. National Advisory Commission on Civil Disorders, Hearings, p. 148.
27. Starr, op. cit., p. 244.
28. Ibid., p. 228.
29. Ibid., p. 255.
30. Personal interview.
31. Spring et al., "Crisis of the Underemployed," p. 53.
32. Wright, *Ready to Riot*, p. 57.
33. Davidoff et al., "Suburban Action: Advocate Planning for an Open Society," p. 12.
34. Personal interview.
35. Hayden, *Rebellion in Newark*, pp. 63-64.

36. U.S. Department of Labor, *Manpower Report of the President,* (April 1972), p. 20.

37. Hayden, *A View of the Poverty Program,* p. 36.

38. Wright, *Ready to Riot,* p. 82.

39. Personal interview.

Chapter 13

1. Meyers, *The Role of the Private Sector in Manpower Development,* p. 85.

2. Wright, *Ready to Riot,* p. 81.

3. "Target: Negro Jobs," p. 22.

4. Research Institute of America, Inc., *What Can You Do About the Hard-Core Unemployed,* p. 4.

5. Remarks made at a conference in Glen Cove, New York, sponsored by Skill Achievement Institute, January 24, 1969.

6. Personal interview.

7. Champagne and King, op. cit., p. 432.

8. U.S. National Advisory Commission on Civil Disorders, Hearings, p. 61.

9. Ibid., p. 77.

10. Brennan, op. cit., p. 157.

11. Taeuber et al., "Occupational Assimilation and the Competitive Process," p. 273.

12. Kalb, "Success in Employing Negroes," p. 199.

13. The Urban Coalition, *Private Industry and the Disadvantaged Worker,* p. 20.

14. Nadeau, *The Black Worker in a Black-Owned Company.*

15. Burack, *Manpower Planning and Programming,* p. 367.

16. "Hiring Is Just the Beginning," p. 47.

17. Becker, op. cit., p. 128.

18. U.S. National Advisory Commission on Civil Disorders, Hearings, p. 183.

19. Research Institute of America, Inc., *What Can You Do About the Hard-Core Unemployed,* p. 16.

20. Sanders, "Industry Gives New Hope to the Negro," p. 194.

21. Ibid., p. 196.

22. "Target: Negro Jobs," p. 21.

23. PBL, A television program shown on Channel 13, NET-TV, May 11, 1969.

24. Burack, op. cit., p. 366.

25. Julius F. Rothman, Address to the Interstate Conference of Employment Security Agencies, September 23, 1970.
26. Personal interview.
27. U.S. Equal Employment Opportunity Commission, *Hearings on Discrimination in White Collar Employment,* p. 499.

BIBLIOGRAPHY

Aiken, Michael, Terman, Louis A., and Sheppard, Harold L. *Economic Failure, Alienation, and Extremism.* Ann Arbor, Michigan: Michigan University Press, 1968.

Alinsky, Saul. "You Can't See the Stars Through the Stripes." *Proceedings of the National Workshop on the Urban Poor: Manpower and Consumer Potentials.* Washington, D.C.: Chamber of Commerce of the United States, March 26-27, 1968.

American Friends Service Committee. *Report on Baltimore Civil Disorders.* Baltimore, Maryland: April 1968.

Anderson, Nels. *Dimensions of Work.* New York: David McKay Company, Inc., 1964.

Anderson, Nels, and Ishwaran, Karlgoudar. *Urban Sociology.* New York: Asia Publishing House, 1965.

"A Time to Listen . . . A Time to Act." *United States Commission of Civil Rights.* Washington, D.C.: United States Government Printing Office, November 1967.

Aumente, Jerome. "The Ghetto is People." *The Nation.* Vol. 205 (November 27, 1967), pp. 555-557.

Baldwin, James. *The Fire Next Time.* New York: Dell Publishing Co., Inc., 1963.

Baltimore Community Relations Commission. *Report of Employ-*

ment Breakdown by Race of Companies Holding City Contracts. Baltimore, Maryland: 1968.

Banfield, Edward C. "Why Government Cannot Solve the Urban Problems." Daedalus. Vol. 97, No. 4 (Fall 1968), pp. 1231-1241.

Beardwood, Roger. "The New Negro Mood." *Fortune.* Vol. 77 (January 1966), pp. 146-151.

Becker, Gary S. *The Economics of Discrimination.* Chicago: The University of Chicago Press, 1957.

Bell, Daniel. "Reflections on the Negro and Labor." *The New Leader.* Vol. XLVI, No. 2 (January 21, 1963), pp. 18-20.

Benedict, Roger W. "Motivating Negroes: Variety of Programs Aimed at Helping Them Help Themselves." *Wall Street Journal,* July 22, 1964, p. 6.

Berger, Bennett. *Working-Class Suburb.* Berkeley and Los Angeles: University of California Press, 1960.

Berger, Peter L. (ed.). *The Human Shape of Work.* New York: The Macmillan Company, 1964.

Berkely, E. P. "People: The New Voice in Renewal." *Architectural Forum.* Vol. 127 (November 1967), pp. 72-77.

Bernstein, Saul. *Alternatives to Violence.* New York: Association Press, 1967.

Blau, Peter M., and Duncan, Otis D. *The American Occupational Structure.* New York: John Wiley and Sons, Inc., 1967.

Blauner, Robert. "Whitewash Over Watts." *Trans-Action.* Vol. 3, (March-April 1966), pp. 3-9.

Bloom, Robert, and Barry, John R. "Determinants of Work Attitudes Among Negroes." *Journal of Applied Psychology.* Vol. 51, No. 3 (June, 1967), pp. 291-294.

Bloomberg, Warner, Jr., and Schmandt, Henry. (eds.). *Power, Poverty, and Urban Policy.* Beverly Hills, California: Sage Publications, Inc., 1968.

"Blow-Up in the Cities." *New Republic.* Vol. 157 (August 5, 1967), pp. 5-7.

Blum, Fred H. *Toward a Democratic Work Process.* New York: Harper, 1953.

Borow, Henry (ed.). *Man in a World at Work.* Boston, Mass.: Houghton Mifflin Company, 1964.

Bradford, Amory. *Oakland's Not for Burning.* New York: David McKay Company, Inc., 1968.

Brayfield, Arthur H., and Wells, Richard V. "Interrelationships Among Measures of Job Satisfaction and General Satisfaction." *Journal of Applied Psychology.* Vol. 41, No. 4 (August, 1957), pp. 201-205.

Brazziel, William F. "Section B: Manpower Training and the Negro Worker." *Journal of Negro Education.* Vol. 35 (Winter, 1966), pp. 83-87.

Brecher, Charles. *Upgrading Blue Collar and Service Workers.* Baltimore, Maryland: The Johns Hopkins University Press, 1972.

Brennan,.Niall. *The Making of a Moron.* New York: Sheed and Ward, 1953.

Brown, Lloyd L. "The Fomented Conflict." *The Nation.* Vol. 208 (February 10, 1969), pp. 179-181.

Brown, Reagan. "A Recipe for Living: How to Avoid the Strangling of Apathy." *Vital Speeches.* Vol. 35 (December 1, 1968), pp. 122-124.

Bullough, Bonnie. "Alienation in the Ghetto." *American Journal of Sociology.* Vol. 72 (1967), pp. 469-478.

Burack, Elmer H. *Manpower Planning and Programming.* Boston, Mass.: Allyn and Bacon, Inc., 1972.

Caldwell, Earl. "Sutton Urges End to Garnishee Law." *New York Times,* August 28, 1967, p. 27:1.

Callender, Eugene S. "Business and the Hard-Core Unemployed: The Ghetto Subcutters." *Personnel.* Vol. 45, No. 4 (July-August 1968), pp. 8-14.

Caplow, Theodore. *The Sociology of Work.* New York: McGraw-Hill Book Co., 1964.

Carmichael, Stokely, Hamilton, Charles, Coles, Robert, and Kozol, Jonathan. "Black Ghettos: The American Nightmare." *The Atlantic.* Vol. 220, No. 4 (October 1967), pp. 97-110.

Carroll, J. Douglas, Jr. *Home-Work Relationships of Industrial*

Workers. (Unpublished doctoral dissertation, Harvard University, 1950).

Cassell, Frank H. "Business and the Community." *Manpower Planning and Programming..* Boston, Mass.: Allyn and Bacon, Inc., 1972.

Chamber of Commerce of Metropolitan Baltimore. *1963-67 Metropolitan Baltimore Growth Patterns.* Baltimore, Maryland.

_____. *Baltimore to 1980: Employment and Income.* Baltimore, Maryland: July, 1965.

Champagne, Joseph E., and King, Donald C. "Job Satisfaction Factors Among Underprivileged Workers." *Personnel and Guidance Journal.* Vol. 45, No. 5 (October, 1967), pp. 429-34.

Chinoy, Ely. *Automobile Workers and the American Dream.* Garden City, New York: Doubleday, 1955.

City of Cleveland. *The Stokes Administration: First Year Report, 1968.* Cleveland, Ohio: 1969.

Clark, Kenneth B. *Dark Ghetto.* New York: Harper, 1965.

Cleeton, Glen U. *Making Work Human.* Yellow Springs, Ohio: The Antioch Press, 1949.

Cleveland Little Hoover Commission. *The Chapla Report on Urban Renewal in the City of Cleveland.* Cleveland, Ohio: November 16, 1966.

Cohen, Wilbur J. "Ending Poverty: Our Will and Our Way." Presented at International Symposium on American Policy toward Poverty at Home and Abroad. (August 21, 1968).

Coles, Robert. "Like It Is in the Alley." *Daedalus.* Vol. 97, No. 4 (fall 1968).

"Communicating With Employees." *Automation.* Vol. 15 (June 1968), pp. 10-11.

"Community Action and Urban Housing." Washington, D.C.: Office of Economic Opportunity, November 1967.

Condon, George E. *Cleveland: The Best Kept Secret.* Garden City, New York: Doubleday and Company, Inc., 1967.

Cunningham, John T. *Newark.* Newark, New Jersey: New Jersey Historical Society, 1966.

Danzig, Fred. "Positive Hiring Policy Emerged as Result of Negro Boycott, says B & B." *Advertising Age*. Vol. 39 (July 22, 1968), p. 3.

Davidoff, Paul, Davidoff, Linda, and Gold, Neil Newton. "Suburban Action: Advocate Planning for an Open Society." *Journal of the American Institute of Planners*. Vol. 36, No. 1 (January 1970), pp. 12-21.

De Christofaro, Ronald R. "Upgrading Job Skills—Recruit or Retrain?" *Automation*. Vol. 14 (April 1967), pp. 70-73.

Dentler, Robert Mackler, Bernard, and Warshauer, Mary Ellen (eds.). *The Urban R's*. New York: Frederick A. Praeger, 1967.

"Dialogue: Corporate Aid vs. Community Control." *New Generation*. Vol. 50, No. 2 (spring 1968), pp. 22-23.

"The Disadvantaged Poor: Education and Employment." *Task Force on Economic Growth and Opportunity*. Chamber of Commerce, 1966, pp. 229-61.

Doeringer, Peter B. "Discriminatory Promotion Systems." *Monthly Labor Review*. Vol. 90 (March 1967), pp. 27-28.

Drake, St. Clair, and Cayton, H. R. *Black Metropolis*. New York: Harper, 1966.

Drucker, Peter F. "Worker and Work in the Metropolis." *Daedalus*. Vol. 97, No. 4 (fall 1968), pp. 1243-1262.

Duhl, Leonard J. (ed.). *The Urban Condition*. New York: Basic Books, Inc., 1963.

Duhl, Leonard J., and Chayes, Antonia Handler. "Developing Human Resources." *Educational Record*. Vol. 45 (1964), pp. 401-07.

Durkin, Roderick. *Breaking the Poverty Cycle: A Strategy and Its Evaluation*. Cambridge, Mass.: Harvard University Press, 1967.

Dynes, Russell R., Clarke, Alfred C., Dinitz, Simon, and Ishino, Iwao. *Social Problems*. New York: Oxford University Press, 1964.

Ellis, William W. *White Ethics and Black Power*. Chicago: Aldine Publishing Company, 1969.

Emery, Paul E., and Blueck, Bernard C., Jr. (eds.). *Poverty and Mental Health.* Psychiatric Research Report No. 21, American Psychiatric Association (January 1967), pp. 55-65.

"Employers in Riot Cities Speak Out on Recruitment and Hiring of Black Workers." *Monthly Labor Review.* Vol. 9 (December 1968), pp. 42-45.

Endleman, Shalom (ed.). *Violence in the Streets.* Chicago, Ill.: Quadrangle Books, 1968.

Ferman, Louis A., et al. (eds.). *Negroes and Jobs.* Ann Arbor, Michigan: University of Michigan Press, 1967.

"Firms Win Riot Damages." *Newsday.* (February 1, 1969), p. 3.

Foley, Eugene P. *The Achieving Ghetto.* Washington, D.C.: The National Press Inc., 1968.

Form, William H., and Miller, Delbert C. *Industry, Labor, and Community.* New York: Harper and Brothers, 1960.

Friedlander, Frank. "Relationship Between the Importance and the Satisfaction of Various Environmental Factors." *Journal of Applied Psychology.* Vol. 49, No. 3 (June 1965), pp. 160-64.

Friedmann, Eugene A., and Havighurst, Robert J. *The Meaning of Work and Retirement.* Chicago, Ill.: University of Chicago Press, 1954.

Garbin, A. P., and Ballweg, John A. "Intra-Plant Mobility of Negro and White Workers." *American Journal of Sociology.* Vol. 71, No. 3 (November 1965), pp. 315-19.

Garrity, John T. "Red Ink for Ghetto Industries." *Harvard Business Review.* Vol. 46, No. 3 (May-June 1968), pp. 4-6.

Gartner, Alan. *Paraprofessionals and Their Performance.* New York: Praeger Publishers, 1971.

————. *Problem Identified, Solution Awry: A Proposal to Refocus Manpower Policy.* New Careers Development Center, New York University. Mimeographed (February 1969).

George, Alexander L. "Political Leadership and Social Change." Vol. 97, No. 4, *Daedalus.* (fall 1968), pp. 1194-1217.

Geschwender, James A. "Negro Education: The False Faith." *Phylon.* Vol. 29, No. 4 (winter 1968), pp. 371-79.

"Ghetto Dwellers May Lose Out on Jobs." *Engineering News-Record.* (August 31, 1967).

Ginzberg, Eli (ed.). *Negro Challenge to the Business Community.* New York: McGraw-Hill, 1965.

Glazer, Nathan, and Moynihan, Daniel Patrick. *Beyond the Melting Pot: The Negroes, Puerto Ricans, Jews, Italians, and Irish of New York City.* Cambridge, Mass.: The M.I.T. Press, 1963.

Goldstein, Ben. "Developing Black Entrepreneurs." *New Generation.* Vol. 50, No. 2 (spring 1968), pp. 6-10.

Goodman, Charles S. "Do the Poor Pay More?" *Journal of Marketing.* Vol. 32, No. 1 (January 1968), pp. 18-24.

Gouldner, Alvin W. *Patterns of Industrial Bureaucracy.* Glencoe, Ill.: Free Press, 1954.

Governor's Select Commission on Civil Disorders. *Report of the Governor's Select Commission on Civil Disorders.* Trenton, New Jersey: 1968.

Greater Cleveland Growth Association. *A Survey of Cleveland's Inner City Manpower Problem.* Cleveland, Ohio: July 30, 1968.

Greater Cleveland Plans for Progress Council. *1967 Negro Employment Breakthrough Survey.* Cleveland, Ohio: 1968.

Greer, Scott. *The Emerging City, Myth and Reality.* New York: The Free Press of Glencoe, Inc., 1962.

Gregory, Dick. *Nigger.* New York: E. P. Dutton and Co., 1964.

―――. *The Shadow That Scares Me.* Garden City, New York: Doubleday and Company, Inc., 1968.

Grier, William H., and Cobbs, Price M. *Black Rage.* New York: Basic Books, Inc., 1968.

Grimshaw, Allen D. (ed.). *Racial Violence in the United States.* Chicago: Aldine Publishing Company, 1969.

"Growing Success of Negro in the U.S." *U.S. News and World Report,* Vol. 63 (January 3, 1967), pp. 54-57.

Guion, Robert M. "Employment Tests and Discriminatory Hiring." *Industrial Relations.* Vol. 5, No. 2 (February 1966), pp. 20-37.

Habbe, Stephen. *Company Experience with Negro Employment.* National Industrial Conference Board, Inc., 1966.

Handlin, Oscar. *The Newcomers.* Garden City, New York: Doubleday and Company, Inc., 1959.

"The Hard-Core Ghetto Mood." *Newsweek.* Vol. 70 (August 21, 1967), p. 31.

Hare, Nathan. "Recent Trends in the Occupational Mobility of Negroes, 1930-1960: An Intra-Cohort Analysis." *Social Forces.* Vol. 44, No. 2 (1965), pp. 166-73.

"Harris Poll After the Riots." *Newsweek.* Vol. 70 (August 21, 1967), pp. 18-19.

Harris, T. G. "Big Business Do-Gooders: Private War on Poverty." *Look.* Vol. 30 (August 9, 1966), pp. 15-19.

Hawley, Amos H. *Human Economy.* New York: The Ronald Press Co., 1950.

Hayden, Tom. *Rebellion in Newark.* New York: Random House, Inc., 1967.

————. *A View of the Poverty. Program.* New York: Youth-Work Institute, 1966.

Heacock, Roland T. *Understanding the Negro Protest.* New York: Pageant Press, Inc., 1965.

"Hearings Before the National Commission on Urban Problems. Vol. 1." May-June 1967. Washington, D.C.: United States Government Printing Office, 1968.

Hentoff, Nat. *The New Equality.* New York: The Viking Press, 1964.

Herbers, John. "Economic Development of Blighted Inner-City Areas Is Running Into Snags." *The New York Times,* Vol. CXVIII, No. 40,643, May 4, 1969, p. 72.

————. "Gains Are Made in Federal Drive for Negro Hiring." *The New York Times.* January 25, 1970, p. 71.

Herman, Melvin, and Munk, Michael. *Decision Making in Poverty Programs.* New York: Columbia University Press, 1968.

Heron, Alexander R. *Why Men Work*. Stanford, California: Stanford University Press, 1948.

Herzberg, Frederick. *Work and the Nature of Man*. Cleveland, Ohio: World Publishing Co., 1966.

Hill, Herbert. "Demographic Change and Racial Ghettos: The Crisis of American Cities." *Journal of Urban Law*. Vol. 44 (winter 1966), pp. 231-85.

Himes, Joseph S. "Some Work-Related Cultural Deprivations of Lower-Class Negro Youths." *Journal of Marriage and the Family*. Vol. 26, No. 4 (November 1964), p. 22-26.

"Hiring Is Just the Beginning." *Current*. Vol. 98 (August 1968), pp. 47-49.

Hodge, Claire C. "The Negro Job Situation: Has It Improved?" *Monthly Labor Review*. Vol. 92, No. 1 (January 1969), pp. 20-28.

Housing Authority of the City of Newark. *Annual Report*. Newark, New Jersey, 1968.

"How Management Can Help the Unemployed Personnel." *Factory*. Vol. 123, No. 12 (December 1965), pp. 56-57.

Hulin, Charles L., and Smith, Patricia C. "A Linear Model of Job Satisfaction." *Journal of Applied Psychology*. Vol. 49, No. 3 (June 1965), pp. 209-16.

Hunter, David R. *The Slums: Challenge and Response*. New York: The Free Press of Glencoe, 1964.

Hunter, Guy (ed.). *Industrialization and Race Relations*. New York: Oxford University Press, 1965.

"Industry Plugs Positive Negro Job Message." *Business Week*. Vol. 1846 (January 16, 1965), p. 34.

Institute of Management and Labor Relations, Rutgers State University, *Newark, New Jersey: Population and Labor Force*. New Brunswick, New Jersey: December, 1967.

Isenberg, Irwin (ed.). *The City in Crisis*. New York: The H. W. Wilson Company, 1968.

Jacobs, Paul. *Prelude to Riot*. New York: Random House, 1966.

Jeffers, Camille. *Living Poor*. Ann Arbor: Ann Arbor Publishers, 1967.

"The Job Makes the Man." *Nation's Business*. Vol. 57, No. 6 (June 1969), pp. 35-40.

Jones, D. G. "An Evaluation of the Socio-Psychological and Socio-Economic Effects of MDTA Training on Trainees in Selected Michigan Programs." *Dissertation Abstracts*. (1967), p. 27 (9-A), 2821-2822.

Jones, Thomas B. *How the Negro Can Start His Own Business*. New York: Pilot, 1968.

Joseph, Stephen M. (ed.). *The Me Nobody Knows*. New York: Hearst Corporation, 1969.

Kafoglis, Madelyn L. "The Economics of the Community Action Program." *Tennessee Survey of Business*. Vol. 3, No. 4 (December 1967), p. 74.

Kalb, W. J. "Hardcore Training: Cautious Success." *Iron Age*. Vol. 201, No. 12 (March 21, 1968), pp. 74-75.

―――. "Success in Employing Negroes." *Iron Age*. Vol. 48, (June 1967), p. 199.

Keil, Charles. *Urban Blues*. Chicago: University of Chicago Press, 1966.

Kessler, Matthew A. "Economic Status of Non-White Workers, 1955-62." *Monthly Labor Review*. Vol. 86, No. 7 (July 1963), pp. 780-88.

Kidder, Alice Handsaker. "Racial Differences in Job Search and Wages." *Monthly Labor Review*. Vol. 91 (July-December 1968), pp. 24-26.

Kifer, Allen. "Changing Patterns of Negro Employment." *Industrial Relations*. Vol. 3, No. 3 (May 1964), pp. 23-36.

Kihss, Peter. "Suburban Jobs Urged for City's Poor." *New York Times,* May 28, 1968, p. 28:1.

Kornhouser, Arthur. "Toward An Assessment of the Mental Health of Factory Workers: A Detroit Study." *Human Organization*. Vol. 21, No. 1 (spring, 1962), pp. 43-46.

Kornhouser, Arthur, Sheppard, Harold L., and Mayer, Albert J.

When Labor Votes. New York: University Books, Inc., 1956.

Kvaracous, William C., Gibson, John S., and Curtin, Thomas J. (eds.). *Poverty, Education and Race Relations: Studies and Proposals.* Boston: Allyn and Bacon, 1967.

LaManna, Richard A. "Value Consensus Among Urban Residents." *Journal of the American Institute of Planners.* Vol. XXX, No. 4 (November 1964), pp. 317-23.

Lefcourt, Herbert M. "Risk Taking in Negro and White Adults." *Journal of Personality and Social Psychology.* Vol. 2, No. 5 (May 1965), pp. 765-70.

Lefkowitz, Joel. "Self-Esteem of Industrial Workers." *Journal of Applied Psychology.* Vol. 51, No. 3 (June 1967), pp. 521-28.

Leggett, John C. *Class, Race, and Labor: Working Class Consciousness in Detroit.* New York: Oxford University Press, 1968.

Lerner, Max. "The Negro American and His City." *Daedalus.* Vol. 97, No. 4 (fall 1968), pp. 1390-1408.

Levine, Aaron. "Citizen Participation." *Journal of the Amercian Institute of Planners* (August 1960).

Levine, Gene. *Workers Vote.* Totowa, New Jersey: The Bedminster Press, 1963.

Levinson, Harry, Price, Charlton R., Munden, Kenneth J., Mandl, Harold J., and Solley, Charles M. *Men, Management, and Mental Health.* Cambridge, Mass.: Harvard University Press, 1966.

Lewis, Oscar. *Study in Slum Culture.* New York: Random House, 1968.

Liebow, Elliot. *Tally's Corner.* Boston, Mass.: Little, Brown & Company, 1966.

Lincoln, Charles Eric. *Sounds of the Struggle: Persons and Perspectives in Civil Rights.* New York: William Morrow and Company, 1967.

Lipsitz, Lewis. "Work Life and Political Attitudes: A Study of

Manual Workers." *The American Political Science Review.* Vol. 58, No. 4 (April 1964), pp. 951-62.

Locke, Alain (ed.). *New Negro: An Interpretation.* New York: Arno Press, 1968.

"Long Thrust Toward Economic Equality." *Ebony.* Vol. 21 (August 1966), p. 38.

Lurie, Melvin, and Rayach, Elton. "Racial Differences in Migration and Job Search: A Case Study." *Southern Economic Journal.* Vol. 23, No. 1 (July 1966), pp. 81-95.

"Luring Business into the Ghettos." *Newsweek.* Vol. 70 (October 16, 1967), p. 77.

Lynn, Frank. "Cleveland's Stokes: How's He Doing?" *Newsday,* April 2, 1969, pp. 10-11.

Marshall, Ray, and Briggs, Vernon M., Jr. "Negro Participation in Apprenticeship Program." *The Journal of Human Resources.* Vol. 2 (winter 1967), pp. 51-69.

Marx, Karl. *Wage-Labour and Capital.* New York: International Publishers Co., Inc., 1933.

Mayfield, Harold. "Equal Opportunity at the Third and Toughest Stage." *Personnel.* Vol. 47, No. 3 (May-June 1970), pp. 8-15.

McAdow, Jerry E. "Aid to Families with Dependent Children— A Study of Welfare Assistance." *Denver Law Journal.* Vol. 44, No. 1 (winter 1967), pp. 102-31.

Mercer, Charles V. "Interrelations Among Family Stability, Family Composition, Residence, and Race." *Journal of Marriage and the Family.* Vol. 29, No. 3 (August 1967), pp. 456-60.

Meyers, Charles A. *The Role of the Private Sector in Manpower Development.* Baltimore, Maryland: The Johns Hopkins Press, 1971.

Miller, S. M. "The Political Potential of Class and Race." *Dissent.* Vol. 11, No. 2 (spring 1964), pp. 212-18.

Miller, S. M., Rein, Martin, Roby, Pamela, and Gross, Bertram N. "Poverty, Inequality and Conflict." *The Annals of the American Academy of Political and Social Science.* Vol. 373 (September 1967), pp. 16-52.

Minuchin, Salvator, Montalvo, Bravlio, Guerney, Bernard G., Jr.,

Rosman, Bernice L., and Schumer, Florence. *Families of the Slums.* New York: Basic Books, Inc., 1967.

Morse, Nancy C., and Weiss, Robert S. "The Function and Meaning of Work and the Job." *American Sociological Review.* Vol. 20, No. 2 (April 1955), pp. 91-98.

Moscovitch, Edward. "Finding Jobs for the Poor." *The New Republic.* Vol. 155 (November 5, 1966), pp. 16-19.

"A Mother Can't Do a Man's Job." *Newsweek.* Vol. 68 (August 22, 1966), pp. 41-42.

Moynihan, Daniel P. *Maximum Feasible Misunderstanding.* New York: The Free Press of Glencoe, 1969.

Mulford, R. H. "The Integrated Work Force: Where are we Now?" *Management Review.* Vol. 55, No. 11 (November 1966), pp. 4-13.

Mumford, Lewis. *The Condition of Man.* New York: Harcourt, Brace and Co., 1944.

Nadeau, Richard P. *The Black Worker in a Black-Owned Company.* Baltimore, Maryland: Skill Upgrading Incorporated, 1969.

Nagie, James J. "Food Units Struggle in Ghettos." *New York Times,* December 1, 1968, III, p. 14:18.

"Negro Business Feels Stresses of Success." *Business Week.* No. 1910 (April 9, 1966), pp. 70-72.

"Negro Business Urged to Expand." *New York Times,* May 22, 1966, p. 71:5.

"Negro Contractors Charge Discrimination." *Engineering News.* Vol. 78 (March 23, 1967), p. 76.

"Negro-Owner and Managed Plant Fills Big Ghetto Need—Jobs." *Modern Manufacturing.* Vol. 1 (September 1968), pp. 80-88.

"Negro Unionists Set Up Alliance." *New York Times,* February 2, 1969, p. 60:1.

"Negro Women Workers in 1960." Women's Bureau, U.S. Department of Labor. Bulletin 287 (1964).

"Negro Workers Move Up to Better Jobs at a Faster Rate, Study Finds." *Wall Street Journal,* February 11, 1969, p. 1:5.

Newcomb, R., and Simmons, M. "Keep Employees Informed." *Advertising Age*. Vol. 39 (January 15, 1968), p. 69.

Northup, Herbert R. "The Racial Policies of American Industry." *Monthly Labor Review*. Vol. 7 (July 1967), pp. 41-43.

Nozza, Peter R. *Better Jobs for Low-Skilled Workers*. Newark, New Jersey: Industrial Training Services, 1969.

Orum, Anthony M. "A Reappraisal of the Social and Political Participation of Negroes." *American Journal of Sociology*. Vol. 72 (1966), pp. 32-46.

Osofsky, Gilbert. *Harlem: The Making of a Ghetto*. New York: Harper and Row, 1966.

Otten, Allen L. "Where the Jobs Are." *Wall Street Journal,* Vol. CLXX, No. 56, September 20, 1967, p. 18.

Oxaal, Ivar. "The Executive Negro." *Saturday Review*. Vol. 5 (July 1, 1967), pp. 47-48.

Parker, S., and Kleiner, R. J. *Mental Illness in the Urban Negro Community*. New York: The Free Press of Glencoe, 1966.

Pearl, Arthur, and Riessman, Frank. *New Careers for the Poor*. New York: The Free Press of Glencoe, 1965.

Pearlin, Leonard P. "Alienation From Work: A Study of Nursing Personnel." *American Sociological Review*. Vol. 27, No. 3 (June 1962), pp. 314-326.

Pettigrew, Thomas F. *A Profile of the Negro-American*. Princeton, New Jersey: D. Van Nostrand Co., Inc., 1964.

Phalon, Richard. "Business Pressing Search for Negroes." *New York Times,* July 28, 1968, III, p. 13:3.

Planning and Research Associates. *Economic Development Study: Mount Vernon Model Neighborhood*. New York, New York: April, 1972.

Price, Daniel O. "Occupational Changes Among Whites and Non-whites With Projections for 1970." *Social Science Quarterly*. Vol. 49, No. 3 (December 1968), pp. 563-72.

Private Industry and the Disadvantaged Worker. New York: The Urban Coalition, January 1969.

"Progress Report: The Negro as a Manager." *Iron Age.* Vol. 198 (August 11, 1966), p. 41.

"Proteus Plans Sea Chief Franchise Operation for Negro Enterprise." *Advertising Age.* Vol. 39 (February 19, 1968), p. 21.

Purcell, Theodore V. *Blue Collar Man.* Cambridge, Mass.: Harvard University Press, 1960.

Rainwater, Lee. "Open Letter on White Justice and the Riots." *Trans-Action.* Vol. 4, No. 9 (September 1967), pp. 22-32.

Rainwater, Lee, and Wancey, W. L. *Moynihan Report and the Politics of Controversy.* Cambridge, Mass.: Massachusetts Institute of Technology Press, 1967.

Report of the National Advisory Commission on Civil Disorders. New York: Bantam Books, Inc., 1968.

Research Institute of America, Inc. *What Can You Do About the Hard-Core Unemployed.* June 18, 1968.

Riessman, Frank. *Strategies Against Poverty.* New York: Harper and Row, 1968.

Riessman, Frank (ed.). *Up From Poverty.* New York: Harper and Row, 1968.

Rohrlich, George F. "Work and Income Policies for the Negro in Urban Slums." *The Social Welfare Forum, 1968.* National Conference on Social Welfare. New York: Columbia University Press, 1968, pp. 78-93.

Rose, Arnold. *Sociology.* New York: Alfred Knopf, Inc., 1956.

Rosenbloom, Richard S., and Marris, Robin (eds.). *Social Innovation in the City: New Enterprises for Community Development.* Cambridge, Mass.: Harvard University Press, 1969.

Ross, Arthur Max. *Employment, Race and Poverty.* New York: Harcourt, Brace and World, 1967.

Ruda, Edward, and Albright, Lewis E. "Racial Differences In Selection Instruments Related to Subsequent Job Performance." *Personnel Psychology.* Vol. 21, No. 1 (spring 1968), pp. 31-41.

Rutledge, Aaron L., and Gass, Gertrude Zemon. *Nineteen Negro*

Men: Personality and Manpower Retraining. San Francisco: Jossey-Bass Inc., 1967.

Sanders, Charles L. "Industry Gives New Hope to the Negro." *Ebony.* (June 1968), pp. 194-202.

Schnapper, Eric. "Notes and Comments—Consumer Legislation and the Poor." *Yale Law Journal.* Vol. 76 (March 1967), pp. 745-792.

Schneider, Eugene V. *Industrial Sociology.* New York: McGraw-Hill Book Co., Inc., 1957.

Semple, Robert B., Jr. "New United States Report Finds Few Negroes in White Collar Jobs." *New York Times,* August 7, 1967, p. 22.

Sexton, Patricia Cayo. *Spanish Harlem: Anatomy of Poverty.* New York: Harper and Row, 1965.

Sheerin, John B. "Was it a Race Riot or Revolution in Brooklyn?" *Catholic World.* Vol. 203 (September 1966), pp. 327-30.

Sheppard, Harold L., and Striner, Herbert E. "Civil Rights, Employment and the Social Status of American Negroes." The W. E. Upjohn Institute for Employment Research, June 1966.

Sherrard, Thomas D. (ed.). *Social Welfare and Urban Problems.* New York: Columbia University Press, 1968.

Shostak, Arthur B. "Promoting Participation of the Poor: Philadelphia's Antipoverty Program." *Social Work.* Vol. 11 (January 1966), pp. 64-72.

Shostak, Arthur B., and Gomberg, William (eds.). *Blue-Collar World.* Englewood Cliffs, New Jersey: Prentice-Hall, 1964.

"A Shrinking Job Market for Negroes?" *Sales Management.* Vol. 98 (March 15, 1967), p. 38.

Silberman, Charles E. *Crisis in Black and White.* New York: Random House, 1964.

————. "Up From Apathy—The Woodlawn Experiment." *Commentary.* Vol. 37 (May 1964), pp. 51-58.

Silbley, John. "Plumbers Scored on Worker Curbs." *New York Times,* February 23, 1969, p. 49.

Simmons, Ozzie G. *Work and Mental Illness.* New York: John Wiley and Sons, Inc., 1965.

Simon, Herbert, A. *The Shape of Automation.* New York: Harper and Row, 1965.

Skill Achievement Institute. *An Analysis of the Short-Range Impact of High Intensity Training.* Lake Success, New York: 1969.

Slaiman, Donald. "Civil Rights in the Urban Crisis." Transcript of Seminar on Manpower Policy and Program held in Washington, D.C., October 19, 1967. Washington, D.C.: United States Government Printing Office, May 1968.

Smigel, Erwin O. (ed.). *Work and Leisure: A Contemporary Social Program.* New Haven, Conn.: College and University Press, 1963.

Sobin, Dennis P. *Dynamics of Community Change: The Case of Long Island's Declining "Gold Coast."* Port Washington, New York: Ira J. Friedman, Inc., 1968.

―――. "Why Increase Citizen Participation Among Ghetto Residents." *Journal of Black Studies* (March 1972), pp. 359-70.

Spring, William, Harrison, Bennett, and Vietorisz, Thomas. "Crisis of the Underemployed." *The New York Times Magazine,* November 5, 1972, pp. 51-60.

Starr. Roger. *The Living End: The City and Its Critics.* New York: Coward-McCann, Inc., 1966.

Stetson, Damon. "Labor Unit Scores Black Capitalism." *New York Times,* February 23, 1969, p. 49.

Suttles, Gerald. "Social Order of the Slum: Ethnicity and Territory in the Inner City." Chicago: University of Chicago Press, 1968.

Taeuber, Alma F., Taeuber, Karl E., and Cain, Glen G. "Occupational Assimilation and the Competitive Process." *The American Journal of Sociology.* Vol. 72, No. 3 (September 1966), p. 273.

Tanner, Daniel, and Tanner, Laura N. "Teacher Aide—A Job For Anyone in Our Ghetto Schools." *Teachers College Record.* Vol. 69, No. 8 (May 1968), pp. 743-51.

"Target: Negro Jobs." *National Affairs.* (July 1, 1968), pp. 21-30.

Task Force on Economic Growth and Opportunity. *The Disadvantaged Poor: Education and Employment.* U.S. Chamber of Commerce.

Tausky, Curt, and Wilson, William J. "Work Attachment Among Black Men." Paper read at the Eastern Sociological Society Meeting, New York, Spring 1969.

Taylor, Frederick. "New Programs Teach Negroes Good English as Second Language." *Wall Street Journal,* January 19, 1966, p. 167.

"Techniques for Breaking Up America's Racial Ghettos." *Journal of Housing.* Vol. 24, No. 9 (October 1967), pp. 505-10.

Toch, Hans. *The Social Psychology of Social Movements.* New York: The Bobbs-Merrill Co., Inc., 1965.

————. *Violent Men: An Inquiry Into the Psychology of Violence.* Chicago: Aldine Publishing Company, 1969.

Turnbull, John G. *The Changing Faces of Economic Security.* Minneapolis, Minn.: The University of Minnesota Press, 1966.

"Twenty Advertisers Use Brochure to Recruit Negro Employees." *Advertising Age.* Vol. 38 (January 9, 1967), p. 10.

"Upgraded Workers." *Wall Street Journal,* May 13, 1969, p. 1.

"Upward Bound: That Tricky Thing Called Motivation." *Economic Opportunity Office.* Item 057-H.

The Urban Coalition. *Private Industry and the Disadvantaged Worker.* January 1969.

"The Urban Crisis: An Analysis, An Answer." *American Federationist.* Vol. 74 (October 1967), pp. 1-8.

U.S. Department of the Army. *Civil Disturbances and Disasters.* (Field Manual). Washington, D.C., March 1968.

U.S. Department of Commerce, Bureau of the Census. *Poverty Areas in the 100 Largest Metropolitan Areas.* Washington, D.C., 1967.

U.S. Department of Commerce, Bureau of the Census, and U.S.

Department of Labor, Bureau of Labor Statistics. *Social and Economic Conditions of Negroes in the United States.* Washington, D.C., 1967.

U.S. Department of Labor, Bureau of Labor Statistics. *Handbook of Labor Statistics.* Washington, D.C., 1967.

U.S. Department of Labor, Bureau of Labor Statistics, and U.S. Department of Commerce, Bureau of the Census. *Recent Trends in Social and Economic Conditions of Negroes in the United States.* Washington, D.C., July 1968.

U.S. Department of Labor, Bureau of Labor Statistics and U.S. Department of Commerce, Bureau of the Census. *Social and Economic Conditions of Negroes in the United States.* Washington, D.C., October 1967.

U.S. Department of Labor, Bureau of Labor Statistics. *The Negroes in the United States.* Washington, D.C., June 1966.

U.S. Department of Labor, Bureau of Labor Statistics. *Newark, New Jersey: Income, Education, and Unemployment.* Washington, D.C., 1963.

U.S. Department of Labor. "Finding Jobs for Negroes: A Kit of Ideas For Management." *Manpower /Automation Research Monograph No. 9.* U.S. Department of Labor, Manpower Administration, Washington, D.C. (November 1968).

U.S. Department of Labor. *Manpower Report of the President.* Washington, D.C., March 1968, April 1968, April 1972.

U.S. Department of Justice, Office of Law Enforcement Assistance. *Detection of Potential Community Violence.* Washington, D.C., 1968.

U.S. Equal Employment Opportunity Commission. *Hearings on Discrimination in White Collar Employment.* New York: January 1968.

U.S. National Advisory Commission on Civil Disorders. *Employment and Manpower Problems in the Cities: Implications of the Report of the National Advisory Commission on Civil Disorders.* (Hearings). Washington, D.C., June 1968.

"Voluntary Associations of Negroes." *American Sociology Review.* Vol. 27 (October 1962), pp. 1-8.

Walton, Clarence C. *Corporate Social Responsibilities.* Belmont, California: Wadsworth Publishing Co., 1967.

Waskow, Arthur I. *From Race Riot to Sit-In.* Garden City, New York: Doubleday and Company, Inc., 1966.

Waterman, Kenneth S. "Local Issues in the Urban War on Poverty." *Social Work.* Vol. 11 (January 1966), pp. 57-63.

"Watts Panel Issues Its Final Report." *New York Times,* Vol. CXVI, No. 40,027, August 27, 1967, p. 62.

Weaver, Robert C. *Negro Labor: A National Problem.* New York: Harcourt, Brace and Co., 1946.

Wellman, David. "A Jobs-for-Negroes Program that Flopped." *Business Management.* Vol. 34 (June 1968), pp. 37-44.

Wetzel, J. R., and Holland, S. S. "Poverty Areas of Our Major Cities; The Employment Situation of Negro and White Workers in Metropolitan Areas Compared in a Special Labor Force Report." *Monthly Labor Review.* Vol. 89 (October 1966), pp. 1105-10.

"What It's Like To Be a Negro in Management." *Business Management.* Vol. 30, No. 1 (April 1966), pp. 60-88.

Wilensky, Harold L. "Class, Class Consciousness and American Workers." *Institute of Industrial Relations Reprint No. 283.* Berkeley: University of California, 1966.

―――. "Work, Careers, and Social Integration." *International Social Science Journal.* (October 1969), p. 544.

Williams, Walter. "Cleveland's Crisis Ghetto." *Trans-Action.* Vol. 4 (September 1967), pp. 33-42.

Willmann, John B. *The Department of Housing and Urban Development.* New York: Frederick A. Praeger, 1967.

Wills, Garry. *The Second Civil War.* New York: The New American Library, 1968.

Wilson, James Q. (ed.). *The Metropolitan Enigma: Inquiries Into the Nature and Dimensions of America's Urban Crisis.* Washington, D.C.: Chamber of Commerce of the United States, 1967.

Woodson, Carter Godwin. *African Heroes and Heroines* (2nd.

ed.). Washington, D.C.: The Associated Publishers, Inc., 1944.

Wright, Nathan, Jr. *Black Power and Urban Unrest.* New York: Hawthorn Books, Inc., 1968.

———. *Ready to Riot.* New York: Holt, Rinehart and Winston, 1968.

X, Malcolm. *The Autobiography of Malcolm X.* New York: Grove Press, 1964.

Zweig, Ferdynand. *The Worker in an Affluent Society.* New York: The Free Press of Glencoe, 1961.

INDEX